Scope, Sequence, and Coordination:

A Framework *for* High School Science Education

1996 Edition

Edited by Bill G. Aldridge

Contributing Editors:

Physics
    Arthur Eisenkraft   Fox Lane High School, Bedford, N.Y.
    John Laffan   Clinton High School, Clinton, N.Y.
    Paul Mirel   Georgetown Day School, Washington, D.C.
    Gerald Wheeler   National Science Teachers Association, Arlington, Va.

Chemistry
    Dorothy L. Gabel   Indiana University, Bloomington, Ind.
    George E. Miller   University of California, Irvine, Calif.
    Gary Freebury   Flathead High School, Kalispell, Mont.
    Jessie M. Jones   Retired Chemistry Teacher, Rocky Mount, N.C.

Biology
    Tom Hinojosa   California SS&C Coordinator, Santa Clara, Calif.
    William George   Georgetown Day School, Washington, D.C.
    Allison Butler   Clinton High School, Clinton, N.Y.
    Jon Fiorella   Fox Lane High School, Bedford, N.Y.

Earth and Space Sciences
    Linda W. Crow   Baylor College of Medicine, Houston, Tex.
    Fred Brumbaugh   NASA Contractor, Houston, Tex.
    Ada Monzon   University of Puerto Rico, San Juan, P.R.
    Philip Sadler   Harvard Center for Astrophysics, Cambridge, Mass.
    Robert Ridky   University of Maryland, College Park, Md.
    Brett Pyle   Grady Middle School, Houston, Tex.

National Science Teachers Association • 1996

Published by
Project on Scope, Sequence, and Coordination
National Science Teachers Association
1840 Wilson Blvd.
Arlington, VA 22201-3000

© 1995, 1996 by the National Science Teachers Association
All rights reserved
Printed in the United States of America
First printing, 1996 edition

Originally published as *A High School Framework for National Science Education Standards,* 1995.

Designed and produced by Nancy Erwin
Cover design by Martha Young

Scope, Sequence, and Coordination is a national curriculum development project for high school science education developed and researched by the National Science Teachers Association and funded by the National Science Foundation under Grant No. ESI-9354085.

Portions of this book are reprinted with permission from *National Science Education Standards.* Copyright 1996 by the National Academy of Sciences. Courtesy of the National Academy Press, Washington, D.C. This permission does not imply endorsement by the National Academy of Sciences, the National Research Council, or the National Science Education Standards Project.

Library of Congress Card Catalog Number: 96-67750
ISBN: 0-87355-142-7
NSTA Stock Number: PB132X

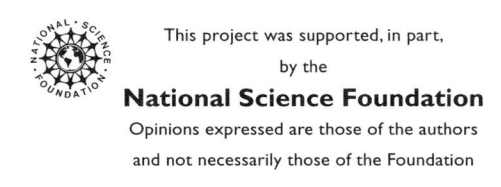

This project was supported, in part, by the
National Science Foundation
Opinions expressed are those of the authors
and not necessarily those of the Foundation

Contents

Preface   v

Introduction   vii

Editoral Note   xi

Part One: Science Subject Matter

    Physics   2
    Chemistry   50
    Biology   84
    Earth and Space Sciences   128

Part Two: Science Applications and Processes

    Unifying Concepts and Processes   162
    Science as Inquiry   167
    Science and Technology   172
    Science in Personal and Social Perspectives   176
    History and Nature of Science   182

Appendix A: Relationship of SS&C to the *NSES*   185

Appendix B: Sample Page from SS&C Matrix   186

Appendix C: Basic Tenets of Scope, Sequence,
    and Coordination   187

Glossary   188

Index of Micro-Units by Subject   192

Index of Micro-Units by Number   201

Preface

In 1992 the project on Scope, Sequence, and Coordination of Secondary School Science (SS&C) published the first of two volumes to guide curriculum designers in planning courses, selecting instructional materials, and constructing assessment instruments according to SS&C principles. That book, *The Content Core*, and a follow-up volume, *Relevant Research*, helped introduce SS&C tenets and principles to middle schools at sites across the country.

In 1995, a third volume—*A High School Framework for National Science Education Standards*—was prepared as a guide to implement, within an SS&C framework, the 1994 draft version of the *National Science Education Standards* being prepared by the National Research Council. This edition, *A Framework for High School Science Education*, is a revision of the original *Framework* based upon input from schools using the 1995 edition and revised to reflect the 1996 final version of the *National Science Education Standards*. Many people have contributed their time and expertise to the development of the original *Framework*, and to this revision. Many more people contributed constructive criticism to the different drafts of this document.

Special thanks is given to SS&C science teachers of the high schools participating in this project:

> Lowell High School, San Francisco, Calif.
> Sherman Indian High School, Riverside, Calif.
> Sacramento High School, Sacramento, Calif.
> Tarboro High School, Tarboro, N.C.
> Northside High School, Pinetown, N.C.
> Georgetown Day School, Washington, D.C.
> Flathead High School, Kalispell, Mont.
> Pleasant Valley High School, Pleasant Valley, Iowa
> North Scott High School, Eldridge, Iowa
> Lee High School, Houston, Tex.
> Yates High School, Houston, Tex.
> Davis High School, Houston, Tex.
> UPR Lab High School, Río Piedras, P.R.
> Fox Lane High School, Bedford, N.Y.
> Clinton High School, Clinton, N.Y.

The SS&C High School Project relies on the dedicated work of the SS&C Project Centers:

> East Carolina University, Greenville, N.C.
> *Charles R. Coble and Jessie Jones, Center Co-Directors*

California Center, Santa Clara, Calif.
Tom Hinojosa, Center Coordinator

Baylor College of Medicine, Houston, Tex.
Linda W. Crow, Center Director

University of Iowa, Iowa City, Iowa
Robert E. Yager, Center Director
Keith Lippincott, School Coordinator

University of Puerto Rico, Río Piedras, P.R.
Manuel Gomez and Acenet Bernacet, Center Co-Directors

Montana State University, Bozeman, Mont.
Gary Freebury, Center Coordinator

The editor expresses special appreciation to Linda W. Crow, Director of the Houston SS&C Center, Martha S. Young, Houston production editor, and Nancy Erwin, SS&C Project Editor. Linda Crow was instrumental in most technical editing of the *Framework* in the areas of earth and space sciences, biology, and chemistry. Nancy Erwin has been responsible for the overall design, editing, and production of this document. Martha Young did much to assist Nancy Erwin in the production work on the components edited in Houston. The Project is also grateful to Phyllis Marcuccio, NSTA Associate Executive Director for Publications, who offered valuable advice on cover style and presentation.

The Project thanks the advisory board:

Albert V. Baez, Vivamos Mejor/USA, Greenbrae, Calif.
Rodney L. Doran, University of Buffalo, Buffalo, N.Y.
Shirley M. Malcom, American Association for the Advancement of Science, Washington, D.C.
Shirley M. McBay, Quality Education for Minorities (QEM) Network, Washington, D.C.
Mary Budd Rowe, Stanford University, Stanford, Calif.
Paul Saltman, University of California–San Diego, La Jolla, Calif.
Kendall N. Starkweather, International Technology Education Association, Reston, Va.
Kathryn Sullivan, Chief Scientist, NOAA, Washington, D.C.

The Project also greatly appreciates the assistance provided by the National Research Council staff, especially that provided by Rick Klausner, Patrice Legro, and Angelo Collins.

Finally, we thank the National Science Foundation for providing the funds that have made this project possible.

Bill G. Aldridge
Editor and
Project Director

Introduction

Since its implementation in 1990, the NSTA-initiated project on Scope, Sequence, and Coordination of Secondary School Science (SS&C) has been successfully introduced at the middle school level at six sites across the country. Building on these middle level experiences, NSTA currently is conducting a carefully focused project to develop and evaluate the SS&C program in grades 9–12. The SS&C High School Project closely adheres to basic SS&C tenets. At the same time, it is designed to enable students to learn the grades 9–12 science specified in the *National Science Education Standards (NSES)* recently developed by the National Research Council (NRC) of the National Academy of Sciences (National Academy Press, Washington, DC, 1996).

Working with the public draft version of *National Science Education Standards* circulated by the National Research Council in November 1994, SS&C project leaders and teachers developed a framework—*A High School Framework for National Science Education Standards* (NSTA, Arlington, VA, 1995). This book is a revision of the *Framework*, having been revised to reflect a year of experience with SS&C in schools, and to reflect a full grades 9–12 sequence for concepts and learning experiences.

The *Framework* is designed to serve as a guide for implementing SS&C at the high school level. Scientists, science education experts, and classroom science teachers have all contributed to the development of the *Framework*, and we believe that it is an extremely useful guide for those who want to reform high school science in accordance with the best research, as reflected in the tenets of SS&C, and who also want their students to achieve national science education standards.

By necessity, this document will undergo further revisions. The sequential nature of this four-year high school project, and the fact that we are now completing work on grade nine and preparing for grade ten, means that grades nine and ten have been addressed with much more consideration than grades eleven and twelve. Additional clarification will occur in future editions of or addendums to the *Framework*.

The *Framework* is ordered by discipline. Part One consists of sections on physics, chemistry, biology, and the earth and space sciences. Within each discipline are listed the topics that compose the standards (such as The Cell; Origin and Evolution of the Universe; etc.). Scientific statements—generalizations—about these topics appear immediately following. With few exceptions, these topics and associated generalizations are taken verbatim from the *NSES*. The exceptions are generalizations that are quite easily and obviously inferred as essential to the understanding of one or more of the *NSES* statements. In such cases we make clear that they are SS&C inferences, and not part of the *NSES*.

Following each generalization, we have provided a more detailed explanation and have identified related concepts, empirical laws or observed relationships, models and theories, and a learning sequence. With the exception of concepts and learning sequence within a given topic, the order in which these framework components are listed, as well as the order of presentation of topics and related generalizations, is unrelated to the order in which SS&C materials should be selected or the material learned. We have, however, attempted to select concepts and specific learning experiences as to their appropriateness for each year of grades nine through twelve.

It is important that readers recognize that listing concepts and other framework components for a particular grade level does not mean that they are learned for the first, or only, time at that level or under that topic exclusively. Many concepts, theories, principles, and laws have been learned over several earlier years and will be revisited later. Likewise, such material may be addressed under several different topics or generalizations. This, of course, reflects basic SS&C tenets regarding sequencing of content and coordination of subjects.

Part Two of the *Framework* consists of the five components of the *National Science Education Standards* that complete the content standards for grades 9–12. These components, reprinted here in their entirety, are *Unifying Concepts and Processes, Science as Inquiry, Science and Technology, Science in Personal and Social Perspectives,* and *History and Nature of Science*. It is important that the subject content standards—*Physical Science, Life Science, and Earth and Space Science* (broken out in this book as *Physics, Chemistry, Biology, and Earth and Space Science*)—be considered in relation to these other, more general, components. The chart in Appendix A shows the relationship of these various components in the SS&C project. Also indicated are the kinds of learning materials being produced.

The most important and significant aspect of the *Framework*, and the one that elicits the most comment, is its level. Many people who look at the *Framework* are concerned that we expect too much of "ordinary" students. This concern reflects a prevalent, but incorrect, belief that only certain individuals can learn science at any significant depth and that they are few in number and uniquely qualified by inherent intellectual aptitude and talent. There is now considerable evidence that this attitude and belief system, though widely held, is based upon faulty data and biased experience. One of the major goals of the SS&C project is to demonstrate that science at a significant level *can* be learned by essentially all students, if the science learning is spread over several years, sequenced properly, and based upon experience with real phenomena. The fundamental goal of SS&C, and the avowed goal of the NRC standards, is to make science understandable and enjoyable for all students.

Appendix C is a list of SS&C tenets. The tenets themselves are extremely important, as they provide the backbone of the project. There is also a glossary following the Appendices. The purpose of the glossary, and of the use of categories like *concepts, empirical laws, models,* and *theories,* is to focus attention on distinctions among these categories, mainly because misconceptions abound regarding such things. For example, $D = M/V$ is often confused by students to mean some kind of natural law, when, in fact, it is a *definition* used to express a concept—that of mass density—quantitatively. Similarly, theories are often imposed on phenomena wherein the actual phenomena are obscured and their interpretation biased. Just because we think our current models or theories are "correct" does not justify imposition of those models onto scientific phenomena. For example, light is not waves! Light is light, which sometimes behaves wavelike and at other times behaves particle-like. The failure to distinguish between models or theories and phenomena leads to apparent contradictions or paradoxes that really reflect the inadequacy of our models, not some paradox or contradiction in the natural world.

How is this book to be used? The *Framework* is to be used by science educators, curriculum development experts in science education, and science teachers working on curriculum development with scientists. Its purpose is to provide further explanation for the national science education standards and to show how science in the four subject matter areas can be spread out, sequenced, integrated, and coordinated over a period of four years of high school. We urge you to examine and use the *Framework*, and as you gain experience, to provide us with information, suggestions, and corrections, either in subject matter or sequence.

The *Framework* has been used by the SS&C High School Project to produce sequences of learning experiences for grades 9–12. These have been placed in a matrix that connects them with the various components of the *NSES*. Appendix B shows a sample page from one of those matrix pages.

Using the sequence of learning experiences illustrated in the matrix, science teachers, teaching scientists, and project staff have produced a series of *micro-units* for use by teachers and students that enable students to achieve the national standards. These micro-units are listed by subject and by number in the indexes. A micro-unit has two parts: a *teacher* section and a *student* section. The teacher materials include what the teacher needs to help students learn the content of that micro-unit, along with assessment items for determining if they have done so. Student materials provide the basic activities and investigations to be carried out by the students, along with readings from a variety of sources appropriate to that unit. Labs and other hands-on activities are open-ended and inquiry based, and readings often include applications in personal and social contexts.

A principal purpose of this project is to establish, through evidence in the form of valid measures of student achievement, that a program based on SS&C tenets, and materials derived from the *Framework* and associated matrix, will better enable a representative sample of high school students to achieve the *NSES* than would traditional instruction with the layer cake curriculum of one year of biology (which 80% now study), one year of chemistry (which 40% now study), and one year of physics (which only 20% now study).

Thirteen high schools having diverse populations and resources are participating in this project, along with suitably identified control classes that utilize traditional curricula. The summative evaluation component of the project—called a *time-lag study*—is being administered and carried out *independently* at the University of Minnesota by Dr. Frances Lawrenz and her staff, with consulting assistance from Dr. Wayne Welch. This time-lag study is funded through NSTA's SS&C project but is otherwise completely independent. Furthermore, Dr. Lawrenz and her staff have *not* relied on the *Framework* to interpret the *NSES*. Instead they have made their own independent interpretation of the standards, and on the basis of that independent interpretation, have created or selected test items and other measures to fairly assess the relative success of SS&C students versus traditional students in achieving the *NSES*. This is a crucially important point. Not only will her study determine whether SS&C students better achieved the *NSES*, but this will be a scientific way of validating SS&C's *Framework* interpretation.

Editorial Note on Micro-Units

Throughout the *Framework* are brief numbered descriptions of the learning experiences that must occur at each grade level, nine through twelve. Each of these descriptions corresponds to a "micro-unit," a collection of carefully selected laboratory activities, readings, and assessment items designed to achieve the *National Science Education Standards*. A micro-unit requires an average of three class periods to complete, and many include "laboratory" activities that can be carried out at home.

Each micro-unit has a teacher version and a student version. The teacher version contains laboratory activities and several assessment items designed to measure depth of understanding of the science being learned in that unit. The student version contains the lab activities, supplemented by questions and problems, and three or more readings.

Usually a micro-unit has redundancy, so that there are a variety of laboratory experiences and readings, allowing the opportunity for a student to focus on areas of personal interest. Also, this redundancy provides emphases on the other *NSES* content standards: S*cience as Inquiry, Science and Technology, Science in Personal and Social Perspectives, and History and Nature of Science.* Appendix B has a sample matrix to show how micro-units emphasize these various standards components. The content standard *Unifying Concepts and Processes* is the basis upon which micro-unit activities are connected, one to the other, in a sequence designed for implementation.

It must be strongly emphasized that neither the standards nor the learning experiences in this book are arranged in the sequence that they would be learned, except by grade level within a standard topic (see the index of micro-units by subject). Such a sequence must be created to achieve the best pedagogical arrangement.

The micro-units produced in SS&C will be available from NSTA on CD-ROM. In addition, through the cooperation of the Microsoft Corporation, you may freely download from the Internet, and use but not sell, copies of these micro-units in Adobe Acrobat PDF format (http://www.gsh.org/NSTA_SSandC). This format was chosen because the Adobe Acrobat reader may be downloaded free from Adobe (http://www.adobe.com), and there is a verison of the reader for any computer platform. Micro-units are offered in three resolutions, and they are at various levels of development, from those "under construction" to those fully developed and revised. If you use one of these micro-units with your students, we would like very much to have corrections, suggestions, etc. You may use the same Internet address to give us that feedback. In this way you can become part of a global development project.

Part One

Science Subject Matter

Physics

Chemistry

Biology

Earth and Space Sciences

Physics

NSES Topics

Motions and Forces

Conservation of Energy and the Increase in Disorder

Interactions of Energy and Matter

Motions and Forces

(*NSES*, pp. 179–181)

Translational Kinematics

SS&C Inferred Generalization (*NSES*, pp. 179–181)
Motions are described quantitatively in science using concepts given the names distance, displacement, speed, velocity, and acceleration. Relationships among these quantities are most easily interpreted and used to solve problems by means of graphical techniques involving slopes and areas under curves.

Further Description:

Before students can understand how a net force is connected to motion, they need to understand how motion is described. This topic is called *kinematics*. Motion in one direction along a straight line involves just the ordinary concept of distance, as might be read on an odometer. For such a motion we can use scalar distances, speeds, and accelerations.

If, however, the motion reverses or changes direction, the concept of distance becomes more complicated. The actual distance along the path would be more than the final straight-line distance from the starting point. In such cases, we need to introduce the concept of *displacement*. For motion along a curved path, we must introduce the concept of a *vector displacement*. However, for motion along a straight line, the plus or minus sign can be used to indicate direction. This approach allows for much of kinematics to be studied before introducing two- or three-dimensional motion, where the vector character of motion becomes essential.

When first studying motion, students must learn the subtle distinctions between time (as a clock reading) and a time interval. They must understand that average speed is a definition of total distance traveled (as might be indicated on an odometer) divided by how long the motion occurs, and not always some average of initial and final values of speed, the way ordinary averages are often computed.

Students need to construct and interpret graphs to learn that the slope of a d-t curve gives speed and that the slope of a v-t curve gives acceleration. They also need to learn that the "area" under a v-t curve gives distance traveled. Using these graphical techniques, they can solve complex motion problems without the use of equations or formulas.

Motions and Forces

TRANSLATIONAL KINEMATICS, CONT.

At the more advanced levels, where there is two- and three-dimensional motion, students learn that we must use displacement, velocity, and vector acceleration (instead of simply distance, speed, and scalar acceleration). They will learn that these quantities do not add, subtract, or multiply using ordinary arithmetic or algebraic operations, and do not even use all of the rules of the arithmetic or algebra of real numbers (vector products are not commutative, for example). Instead, they must use vector arithmetic and algebra. This mathematics motion along curved paths is described quantitatively, like motion along circular or parabolic paths, and it leads to concepts like *centripetal acceleration*.

Students must also learn that complex motions can be considered by examining *components* along the axes of a coordinate system, recognizing that motion along the x, y, and z axes can be considered independently of one another. For example, motion in two dimensions can be considered as two one-dimensional problems using scalars; then the motion can be considered again as a vector using these two components. This is especially important in describing projectile motion and in understanding the concepts of a *reference frame* and *relative velocity*.

In working with slopes of a d-t or v-t graph to arrive at speeds or accelerations when speed in the case of a d-t curve, or acceleration in the case of the v-t curve, is not constant, we must take very small intervals of time to approximate a tangent to the curve. This, of course, was the problem that led Newton to invent differential calculus. A derivative finds the slope in the limit as the time interval approaches zero in its duration.

Concepts Needed:

Grade 9
Instant in time (clock reading), interval of time, reference point, position, distance, change in position, average speed, instantaneous speed (as a speedometer reading only), average acceleration

Grade 10
Air resistance, reference frame, projectile motion, circular motion, centripetal acceleration

Grade 11
Vector displacement, velocity, instantaneous velocity, change in velocity, acceleration and instantaneous acceleration

Motions and Forces

TRANSLATIONAL KINEMATICS, CONT.

Grade 12
Combining vector quantities, vector components,

Empirical Laws or Observed Relationships:
"Area" under a speed vs. time (v-t) curve gives distance, if motion is in one direction along a path. If the direction reverses during the motion, the "area" under the velocity vs. time curve gives the displacement. Similarly, for motion in one direction along a path, the slope of a distance vs. time (d-t) curve gives speed, and the slope of a speed vs. time curve gives the scalar acceleration along the path. But if the motion involves a direction reversal, the slope of a displacement time graph gives the velocity, and the slope of a velocity time graph gives the acceleration (as a vector).

Theories or Models:
Model of an extended object moving, but represented by a particle (point) in motion

Learning Sequence, Grades 9–12:
Grade 9
Micro-Unit 914(a). Students should learn the quantitative aspects of motion along a straight line. They should recognize situations involving acceleration or constant velocity by analyzing ticker tape strips or strobe photos. In this regard they should learn to use average speed and the acceleration for cases of uniform acceleration.

Students should explore qualitatively the acceleration due to gravity as a phenomenon but not yet try to measure it. They should be encouraged to offer hypotheses to explain gravity, understanding that naming it does not explain it. They should be able to describe motion in one dimension using a d-t graph and constant speed and uniformly changing speed (constant acceleration) using a v-t graph. They should also be able to interpret such graphs.

Micro-Unit 915. Students could compare accelerating a bowling ball along a straight-line path with the experience of trying to keep the ball moving in a circular path by pushing on it with a broom. Also, when accelerating in the forward direction in a car, students experience being "pushed backward" (the fictitious *inertial force*) against the car seat. They learn that this is their inertia: the car moves forward, and they tend to remain at rest until the car seat pushes them forward.

Motions and Forces

TRANSLATIONAL KINEMATICS, CONT.

Micro-Unit 923. In a similar way students can think of moving around a curve, where they feel pushed outward (the fictitious *centrifugal force*). They can connect their experience on a curve with their forward experience and use the same explanation. Their inertia would have them continue in a straight line, but the car seat or door pushes them toward the center of a circle (of which the curve over which they are traveling is a small arc). Thus it is a centripetal, not a centrifugal, acceleration. Students could try this while carrying a bubble accelerometer to convince themselves that the acceleration is toward the center of the circle.

Relative velocity could be considered from the standpoint of two parallel axes in one dimension, tapping students' experience of two moving trains or cars.

Grade 10

Micro-Unit 1010. Students should learn to measure speeds and accelerations quantitatively using any of various displacement timing methods. The acceleration due to Earth's gravity should be measured at this time. They should learn to convert d-t graphs to v-t graphs for motion with constant velocity. Mathematical and graphical interpretations of average velocity should be addressed.

Students should investigate the independence of perpendicular motions. Examples can include crossing a river (nonaccelerated perpendicular motion) and the falling of two balls, one with an initial horizontal velocity (accelerated vertical motion and independent horizontal motion).

Students should investigate relative velocity. At this time the use of vectors should be limited to one-dimensional motion (scalar addition) and, for two dimensions, mutually perpendicular motion (Pythagorean addition).

Micro-Unit 1021(a). Students should investigate qualitatively the resistance to motion that is presented by fluids—air in particular. Experiments with simple parachutes can be useful. They should be guided to recognize that the interaction with air of an object falling due to gravity may influence the results of their measurement of that acceleration, but they should see that neglecting this frictional effect and idealizing the results makes investigating acceleration due to gravity easier. They could then be challenged as to how this experiment would work differently on the moon. This would allow problem solving for motion in Earth's gravity.

Motions and Forces

TRANSLATIONAL KINEMATICS, CONT.

Grade 11

Micro-Unit 1117. The quantitative concepts of vector displacement and average velocity should be introduced and used. Vectors and simple vector addition and subtraction should be used for displacements, average velocities, and in the case of circular motion, to arrive at the centripetal acceleration.

Projectile motion should be examined from the standpoint of vector components, and students should learn how to resolve vectors into their components in three dimensions. They should learn how to derive the equation for centripetal acceleration without the use of vectors and then with the use of vectors.

Grade 12

Micro-Unit 1210. Students should study quantitatively changes in velocity and displacement from one reference frame to another. Instantaneous speeds and scalar accelerations can be considered using slopes at a point as determined by the concept of a first derivative. The extension to the vector limits can also be carried out. In the case of "areas" under curves, students who have had some experience with calculus could use integrals to provide "distances." For students with access to computers, simple algorithms could be used to carry out numerical integration and the concept introduced in that way.

When addition of relative velocities is introduced, students will become aware of problems that are consequences of the first postulate in special relativity—nothing travels faster than light.

Rotational Kinematics

SS&C Inferred Generalization (*NSES*, pp. 179–181)

The rotational motion of ideal rigid objects can be described using angle of rotation in radians, angular speed, and angular acceleration. Methods of use and analysis are mathematical analogs to translational kinematics, so that many of the same methods are applicable.

Further Description:

Exploring the rotational motion of rigid objects begins with reviewing the motion of a point object moving in a circular path of radius r. The basic concepts of angular "distance," angular speed, and angular acceleration can be developed for this simple model.

Motions and Forces
ROTATIONAL KINEMATICS, CONT.

Next we can consider ideal rigid bodies of extended size, probably symmetrical in shape like rotating cylinders, and for simplicity we should consider only those cases where there is rotation about an axis of symmetry. The fixed axis of rotation is then defined, and we can introduce the direction of angular displacement as a vector.

The angular velocity is also a vector. This vector character is introduced mainly because the components of angular momentum vectors are used for electron revolution (angular momentum quantum number) and rotation (spin quantum number) in quantum chemistry. Angular accelerations can then be considered.

The kinematics of angular motion of rigid objects is often an analog of the translational motion case and therefore can be easily considered. The angular motion of solid objects about a simply determined axis fixed in space could lead to consideration of motion of nonsymmetrical objects about some axis, particularly in *qualitative* discussions.

Concepts Needed:
Grade 9
Rotation (in revolutions), angular speed (in revolutions/sec), frequency (in revolutions/sec), period (time per revolution)

Grade 10
Frequency f in Hz, period, t or T as reciprocal of f

Grade 11
Axis of rotation, radian as measure of angular displacement, θ, s/r, angular velocity, ω, as v/r

Grade 12
Angular acceleration, α; frequency f or ν (as $\omega/2\pi$);

Empirical Laws or Observed Relationships:
"Area" under an angular speed vs. time curve gives angular displacement. Slope of angular displacement vs. time curve gives angular velocity. Slope of angular velocity vs. time curve gives angular acceleration.

Theories or Models:
The model of an extended rigid object must be considered from the standpoint of the axis of rotation and the reference lines needed to measure angular motion.

Motions and Forces

ROTATIONAL KINEMATICS, CONT.

Learning Sequence, Grades 9–12:

Grade 9

Micro-Unit 920. Using motion of objects about fixed axes or point masses moving in circular paths, students should describe such rotation using only revolutions for angular displacement, rev/sec for angular speed, and sec/rev for period.

Grade 10

Micro-Unit 1015(a). Circular motion should be analyzed to establish the concepts of linear speed, period, and frequency of rotation.

Micro-Unit 1016(b). Rotational inertia can be introduced as the tendency to resist changes in rotational motion, but it should not be developed further at this grade level.

Grade 11

Micro-Unit 1118. Students should explore the concept of a radian and why such a measure is needed to measure angular "distance." The vector character of angular displacement, angular velocity, and angular acceleration can be introduced.

Grade 12

Micro-Unit 1212. At this level, students discover that angular displacements, other than for infinitesimal amounts, are not vectors. They are not commutative in addition, as vectors must be. (Rotate a book about each of two nonparallel axes, then do it again in the opposite order.) These concepts can then be applied to symmetrically shaped objects rotating about an axis, like cylinders.

The angular motion of systems should be examined. Also, gyroscopic motion, inertial guidance systems, and gyroscopic effects in bicycles, airplanes, and engine flywheels could be considered.

Motions and Forces
DYNAMICS AND NEWTON'S LAWS OF MOTION

Dynamics and Newton's Laws of Motion

NSES Generalization (pp. 179–180)

Objects change their motion only when a net force is applied. Laws of motion are used to calculate precisely the effects of forces on the motion of objects. The magnitude of the change in motion can be calculated using the relationship F = ma, which is independent of the nature of the force. Whenever one object exerts force on another, a force equal in magnitude and opposite in direction is exerted on the first object.

Further Description:

Kinematics *describes* how things move but not why. With an understanding of kinematics, students can describe motion of various kinds. But *why* do objects move in ways that they do? What accounts for the changes in their motion? This is called *dynamics*.

Galileo's law of inertia—an object at rest remains at rest, and one in motion in a straight line at constant speed continues in that same motion—is equivalent to Newton's first law. Students must observe that to change either the speed of an object or its direction of motion, there must be an interaction of the object with something else. That interaction is called a *force*. In its simplest description, force is just a pull or push, but in general it is a measure of the interaction between the objects. Force can be defined operationally in terms of the stretch of a linear spring. Objects can be made to speed up, slow down, or change their direction of motion by means of an unbalanced force, i.e., a net force.

Students are familiar with mass as something proportional to the amount of substance and as something they measure with a balance. The acceleration of an object is inversely proportional to its mass when a net force acts. The property of a mass resisting changes in motion is called inertia. Sometimes people refer to gravitational mass as the kind measured on a balance and inertial mass as the kind that opposes acceleration. Although these two kinds of mass need not be the same, Einstein postulated that they are equivalent, and all subsequent experiments have verified this equivalence.

Newton's second law, $F = ma$ (where F must be the net force), expresses the relationship between the net force acting on a mass and its acceleration. When considering forces, care must be taken to identify all of the forces acting upon that object, and the sum of these forces must be a vector sum. This vector sum must be used to find the resulting vector acceleration.

Motions and Forces

DYNAMICS AND NEWTON'S LAWS OF MOTION, CONT.

In the process of identifying forces acting on an object, we encounter forces acting on that object and forces it exerts on other things. This observation leads to another of Newton's laws, Newton's third law of motion—forces come in pairs, sometimes expressed "for every action there is an equal and opposite reaction." If you push on something, it pushes back on you with an equal and oppositely directed force. Newton's laws allow us to predict the motion of an object if we know the forces acting on the object and its initial motion. We need only find the acceleration, then use kinematics to describe the motion.

Since there is a constant acceleration of freely falling bodies close to Earth's surface, with g as the value of that acceleration, there must be a constant force. This force is called the weight of the body and is given by w = mg. The fact that Earth is not touching the falling body until it hits the ground illustrates another important idea, force acting at a distance but not touching.

An object moving in a circle (even at a constant speed, since the direction of motion is continuously changing) is accelerating, as we have previously shown, so there must also be a center-directed force—a centripetal force. And some source of this centripetal force must be present. In the case of uniform circular motion, the force produces only a change in direction, not a change in speed. This motion is an example of what happens when a force is applied at right angles, or orthogonal, to the velocity. When two orthogonal forces act on an object, the change in motion caused by one force is independent of the change in motion caused by the other force.

Concepts Needed:

Grade 9
Gravitational mass, force exerted by things touching or by things acting at a distance

Grade 10
Inertial mass, newton as a unit of force, net force or unbalanced force, action force, reaction force, weight as a force

Grade 11
Normal force, force equilibrium, resistive force (by contact at rest or by rubbing and plowing through)

Grade 12
Vector force, free-body diagram, orthogonal forces (forces at right angles to each other and their effects on motion), centripetal force (and source of a given centripetal force, i.e., gravity, contact, friction, electric, magnetic)

Motions and Forces

DYNAMICS AND NEWTON'S LAWS OF MOTION, CONT.

Empirical Laws or Observed Relationships:

Whenever two objects interact with each other (regardless of the source of that interaction), they both accelerate during the interaction. Furthermore, during the interaction the ratio of the magnitude of the two accelerations is equal to the reciprocal of the ratio of their masses. This means that during that interaction, each object accelerates by an amount that is inversely proportional to its mass. It is also observed that these accelerations are oppositely directed.

Theories or Models:

Newton recognized that the observed empirical relationship of two interacting objects, $m/M = A/a$, equivalent to $ma = MA$, is independent of the nature of the interaction. That interaction was therefore called a force. Newton's law, using the concept of force for the interaction, is a theory expressed by $F = ma$. Similarly, Newton's first law is merely a special case of $F = ma$, when the net force is zero. In that case, the acceleration must also be zero, which means that the object is at rest or moving with a constant velocity. Newton's third law expresses the character of the accelerations of interacting objects by recognizing that the two forces, each acting on the other, must have the same value but be oppositely directed.

Learning Sequence, Grades 9–12:

Grade 9

Micro-Unit 916. Students should first consider the qualitative aspects of forces and changes in motion, gaining experience with force as push and pull. They should then consider simple interactions and observe equal and opposite forces by pulling on pairs of connected spring scales. Observing motion under nearly frictionless conditions, they will see evidence of Newton's first law.

Micro-Unit 918. Students should use spring balances to measure forces and, using cart and spring scales, observe the motion of objects of different mass under the action of the same force. With these observations, students will gain a qualitative understanding of Newton's second law.

Grade 10

Micro-Unit 1011. Students should acquire the concept of inertial mass using an inertial balance to compare masses, and learn to measure weight in Newtons. They should carry out experiments with interacting objects to observe the relationship of mass to acceleration during an interaction. They can then use Newton's laws to determine the motion of objects under a constant force along a straight line. They must be able to identify all forces

Motions and Forces

DYNAMICS AND NEWTON'S LAWS OF MOTION

acting on an object in one-dimensional motion, find the acceleration given the net force, and describe the motion or change in motion.

At this level, vectors are not used, but plus and minus to indicate direction serves as a precursor to later use of vectors. The distinction between weight and mass should be addressed. Students should learn that weight on Earth is the force due to gravity that accelerates objects downward. Knowing the acceleration due to gravity on Earth, they are able to calculate the weight of an object as a force in newtons.

Grade 11

Micro-Unit 1119. Students should learn to use free-body diagrams to identify forces on an object, including normal forces, and be able to distinguish clearly between forces acting on an object and those exerted by the object internally and on external objects. They can determine that objects are in equilibrium as a consequence of zero net force from several different forces acting on the object at the same time.

Using vector addition of perpendicular forces, students should extend Newton's second law to two dimensions. Treatment should be limited to Pythagorean addition. They should be able to relate centripetal acceleration to centripetal force.

Grade 12

Micro-Unit 1213. Students should use Newton's laws in two dimensions, expressing force and acceleration as vectors. They should learn to sum forces through vector addition and to determine motion or changes in motion in two dimensions.

Students should use vector forces in circular motion and vector forces in projectile motion to determine accelerations. Also, they should be able to resolve vector forces into components and use these components to solve motion problems. They need to solve problems involving several forces acting on an object, determining their magnitude and direction in each case and finding their vector sum. They can then determine the acceleration of the object with Newton's second law and describe the resulting motion.

Motions and Forces
CONSERVATION OF MOMENTUM

Conservation of Momentum

SS&C Inferred Generalization (NSES, pp. 179–181)
During the interaction of two systems, A and B, the force exerted by A on B is equal and opposite to the force exerted by B on A. Since the duration of the interaction provides the time interval, and the forces are equal in magnitude, the changes in momentum of the two systems must also be identical, but oppositely directed. The total momentum must therefore remain the same. This is the **law of conservation of momentum.**

Further Description:
During the time of an interaction between two objects, the forces acting between the objects may be of various kinds: contact, gravitational, electrical, or even nuclear. Contact forces are fundamentally electrical in nature. Similarly, elastic forces, like those exerted by a rubber band or spring, are electrical. Molecular forces are also electrical.

During an interaction, Newton's third law requires that the impulse delivered by one system be equal and opposite to the impulse delivered by the other system. This behavior requires that the magnitude of the change in momentum of each system be the same. Since they are oppositely directed, their sum is zero. In two or three dimensions, where there are three or more interacting systems, the sum must be a vector, where the vector represents the total of the momenta of the interacting systems.

The law of conservation of momentum is one of the major laws of nature, and for any closed system that includes all interacting objects it always holds. Thus, regardless of the nature of the force and of other constraints on objects in the system, like energy considerations, the total momentum is conserved. If there is a net external force on the system, then the total momentum of the system changes at a rate equal to that force. This law is of great interest in applications like sports, safety devices for cars and planes, rockets, and jet propulsion.

Observationally, the total momentum after an event occurs in a closed system equals its total momentum before the event, but only within the uncertainty of measurement.

Concepts Needed:
Grade 9

Interaction, action at a distance

Grade 10

Action and reaction pairs, impulse and momentum

Motions and Forces

CONSERVATION OF MOMENTUM, CONT.

Grade 11
Vector momenta and impulse (two dimensions), system

Grade 12
Free-body diagrams, three-dimensional vector momenta and impulse

Empirical Laws or Observed Relationships:
Newton's third law, law of conservation of momentum

Theories or Models:
Physical systems and free-body diagrams

Learning Sequence, Grades 9–12:

Grade 9
Micro-Unit 917. At this level, students learn to distinguish between forces acting on an object and forces exerted by the object. They need to examine pairs of real objects, identifying the forces on each object and their points of application and direction. They should consider qualitative questions or problems, like the horse-cart "paradox." A qualitative understanding of single mass emission rockets should be developed. These are best illustrated with "exploding carts" of different masses.

Grade 10
Micro-Unit 1012. Students should investigate momentum conservation in one-dimensional interactions. They should begin to examine problems involving collisions of two objects along a straight line in terms of momentum transfer, leading to the law of conservation of momentum. The qualitative concepts of impulse and momentum should be learned.

Grade 11
Micro-Unit 1121. Force transducers connected to a computer can provide graphs of F vs. t, and impulse can be directly observed quantitatively. Students are now ready for collisions in two dimensions and the vector character of momentum. They can also use free-body diagrams in action-reaction problems in two dimensions and solve some problems associated with rockets and propulsion systems.

Grade 12
Micro-Unit 1234. Students can now consider conservation of momentum involving more than two objects and momentum associated with waves and fields. They should begin a *qualitative and descriptive* approach to interactions

Motions and Forces

CONSERVATION OF MOMENTUM, CONT.

between fields and particles. The uncertainty of momentum and position could also be brought into the discussion at this level. Collisions of elementary particles use momentum conservation to uncover properties of those particles (here relativistic equations are required).

Rotational Dynamics and Angular Momentum

SS&C Inferred Generalization (NSES, pp. 179–181)

When a force acting on an object has the effect of producing a rotation, the resulting angular motion often can be attributed to a quantity called torque, and the laws of that motion are somewhat analogous to Newton's laws for translational motion. (The analogy is not exact or general, since the rotational inertia, I, is, in general, a tensor, whereas mass, m in Newton's law, is a scalar; thus, the two relationships cannot be exact analogs.) When more than one torque acts on an object and they sum to zero, the system is said to be in rotational equilibrium.

Further Description:

Forces acting on real extended objects seldom produce only translational motion. There is very often rotation along with translation. When both are present, the motion is more complicated than when there is simple rotation about a fixed axis or simple translation along a straight line. For many systems and motions, there is a mathematical analogy between rotational and translational motion, with force being analogous to torque and rotational inertia being analogous to mass.

The vector character of torque is essential when examining a two- or three-dimensional situation. The importance of angular momentum and its conservation is directly associated with the concepts of angular impulse and changes of angular momentum. Quantum physics depends strongly on the concept of angular momentum, and at the macroscopic level, the precession of tops and the function of inertial guidance systems are related to these concepts.

Concepts Needed:

Grade 9

Fulcrum, levers

Grade 10

Moment arm, center of gravity, center of mass

Motions and Forces
ROTATIONAL DYNAMICS AND ANGULAR MOMENTUM, CONT.

Grade 11
Torque, rotational inertia, angular momentum

Grade 12
Angular acceleration, spin, angular momentum

Empirical Laws or Observed Relationships:
The relationship of angular acceleration to torque and rotational inertia (torque = angular acceleration × rotational inertia)

Theories or Models:
Conservation of angular momentum

Learning Sequence, Grades 9–12:
Grade 9
Micro-Unit 935(b). At this level, students should learn the basic concepts of a fulcrum and lever.

Grade 10
Micro-Unit 1016(a). Students should observe that a force at right angles to a moment arm tends to produce rotation. Since they will not yet understand rotational inertia, they can at best offer their own hypotheses for this phenomenon. They should observe the *phenomenon* of conservation of angular momentum in situations like the ice skater who brings arms in close or moves them outward.

There are several other phenomena associated with rotational dynamics, phenomena observed using tops and bicycles, that allow *qualitative* understandings of important aspects of rotational dynamics before the introduction of quantitative material in later grades.

Grade 11
Micro-Unit 1126. At this level, students can learn to determine a moment arm and torque and solve simple rotational problems. The concept of rotational inertia as an analog to mass can be developed, with formulas for moments of inertia for simple solids provided but not derived. Applications to engine flywheels, especially to composite flywheels used for energy storage, can be considered.

Grade 12
Micro-Unit 1235. The vector character of angular momentum needs to be considered at this level. Precession of tops can be brought into the discus-

Motions and Forces

ROTATIONAL DYNAMICS AND ANGULAR MOMENTUM, CONT.

sion, as well as inertial guidance systems. The most important reason for learning rotational motion in its vector characterization is its use in quantum physics and chemistry, where quantum numbers are specified in terms of projections of angular momentum vectors.

Gravitational Force: The Law of Universal Gravitation

NSES Generalization (p. 180)

Gravitation is a universal force that each mass exerts on any other mass. The strength of the gravitational attractive force between two masses is proportional to the masses and inversely proportional to the square of the distance between them.

Further Description:

The acceleration of objects in free-fall near the surface of Earth is constant for a given location and nearly constant (within 0.5%) everywhere on Earth. This is called the *acceleration due to gravity*.

Like all other forces, that which produces the change in motion under the gravitational interaction follows Newton's second law. The gravitational force is a force whose form can be determined by considering the motion of planets about the sun or satellites moving around a planet or about Earth. Through Kepler's empirical laws, and Newton's second law of motion (through its application to motion of an orbiting body moving in an elliptical orbit), one can determine that the force between planets and the sun is an inverse square law force that is proportional to the product of the interacting masses and inversely proportional to the square of their separation. This force law is called the *law of universal gravitation*.

For spherically symmetric objects, the separations can be measured from the centers. But how do we know this? Newton asked the same question. He assumed that for arbitrarily shaped objects, the separation could be determined only by summing all forces from each pair of point masses in each of the two interacting objects. This, of course, is what Newton did in developing the universal law of gravitation. He invented the integral calculus to carry out those summations. (In Germany, Leibniz independently invented calculus, and his notation is that commonly used today.)

Newton used his own second law of motion, his third law, along with the empirical laws of Kepler to create the theory of universal gravitation. Through his invention of integral calculus, he could sum the forces from every pair of mass points in Earth and every pair of mass points in the moon to show

Motions and Forces

GRAVITATIONAL FORCE: THE LAW OF UNIVERSAL GRAVITATION, CONT.

that the separation needed was between their centers. We so often use the law of universal gravitation for extended objects that are *not* spherically symmetric, we forget that in doing so we are simply taking advantage of the fact that the objects are so small relative to Earth and its diameter that we can measure separation from its center of mass without introducing error.

For many symmetrical objects the forces between them using the distance between their centers of mass do *not* follow the simple inverse square law. For example, consider a bell bar and a sphere, aligned so that the masses at each end of the bell bar and the sphere are along the same line and the distance from the center of the sphere to the center of mass of the bell bar is the same as the length of the bell bar. The actual gravitational force is 4.44 times larger than would be calculated using the separation between their centers of mass in a simple inverse square law.

The Cavendish experiment demonstrates that such gravitational forces are exerted between ordinary-size objects, things other than planets and the sun or planets and their moons. Through such an experiment, the universal gravitational constant, G, can be determined in the laboratory. Whereas G is universal and constant, g, the measurement of acceleration due to gravity on a planet (which is also a measure of the gravitational field) varies and is dependent upon the planet, its mass, and its radius.

Concepts Needed:

Grade 9
Gravity, point mass, weight as force

Grade 10
Ellipse, perihelion, aphelion, period, inverse square relationship

Grade 11
Spherical symmetry, extended mass, center of mass

Grade 12
Accelerating frame of reference, gravitational field vector

Empirical Laws or Observed Relationships:

Kepler's laws: the law of equal areas in equal times; the fact that planets and moons travel in elliptical orbits; and, most importantly, the constant relationship between the square of the period of a planet and the cube of its average separation from the sun (where this average separation is defined as the average of the perihelion and aphelion, which is the same as the semimajor axis of the elliptical orbit).

Motions and Forces

GRAVITATIONAL FORCE: THE LAW OF UNIVERSAL GRAVITATION, CONT.

Theories or Models:
The law of universal gravitation, the gravitational field, Newton's laws of motion

Learning Sequence, Grades 9–12:

Grade 9
Micro-Unit 914(b). At this level, students should have observed that objects dropped from rest accelerate and that to do so requires some downward push or pull. That downward push or pull for free-fall can, at this point, be given the name *gravity*. It is important that students understand that *naming* the force does not tell anything about it.

Grade 10
Micro-Unit 1014. Students should understand the properties of a geometrical ellipse (by creating simple ellipses with string and pins). Even though Earth's motion about the sun is very nearly circular, they should understand the empirical evidence that this motion is elliptical. (Photographs of the sun show that its apparent diameter changes over a year, and data from a series of such photos can be used in a simulated situation only with an ellipse.)

Students should use the acceleration of gravity, g, for problems in various circumstances on Earth and on the moon and use proportions when applying the law of universal gravitation.

Grade 11
Micro-Unit 1122. Students should determine when objects are in equilibrium as a consequence of zero net force due to several forces and find the value of the gravitational field for various planets and moons about planets.

They should understand how the empirically determined Kepler laws along with Newton's second law applied to centripetal force lead to the law of universal gravitation.

Grade 12
Micro-Unit 1236. Students should use vector forces in circular and projectile motion to determine accelerations and learn to use the concept of a vector field (g as a vector). They should consider complex dynamics problems associated with planetary systems. They should also compare the effects of an accelerating frame with the gravitational field.

Motions and Forces
ELECTRIC FORCE /COULOMB'S AND GAUSS'S LAWS

Electric Force/Coulomb's and Gauss's Laws

NSES Generalization (p. 180)
The electric force is a universal force that exists between any two charged objects. Opposite charges attract while like charges repel. The strength of the force is proportional to the charges, and, as with gravitation, inversely proportional to the square of the distance between them.

Further Description:
Electric charge must be defined in terms of observations of interactions of charged objects. It is quite remarkable that in this high-technology age, the negative charge is still *defined* as the charge given to a rubber rod that has been rubbed with fur, and a positive charge is still defined as the charge given to a glass rod that has been rubbed with silk.

The nuclear model of the atom allows us to create a model of electricity based upon electrons, protons, and ions. Explanations can then be made in terms of these ideas. The chain of evidence up to and including Millikan's experiment and the work leading to Coulomb's and Gauss's laws are fundamental.

Concepts Needed:
Grade 9
Electroscope, charge, electrostatics, conductor, insulator

Grade 10
Galvanometer, induction, polarization, ground

Grade 11
Charges on fundamental particles, electron, proton, neutron, ion, coulomb

Grade 12
Polarization as a vector, vector electric fields

Empirical Laws or Observed Relationships:
There are only two kinds of electric charge, which we define as plus and minus; opposite charges attract and like charges repel; electrically induced polarization; induction; the force between two point charges (or charges on spherically symmetric objects) is inversely proportional to separation and directly proportional to the product of their charges; electric charge is quantized, the electronic charge being the smallest *stable* electric charge found in matter; conservation of electric charge

Motions and Forces

ELECTRIC FORCE / COULOMB'S AND GAUSS'S LAWS, CONT.

Theories or Models:
Rutherford model of an atom, Gauss's law

Learning Sequence, Grades 9-12:

Grade 9
Micro-Unit 943(b). At this level, students should review fundamental observations of electric charge and develop an understanding of how we know that there are only two kinds of electric charge. They should observe that two objects of the same material treated the same way to become charged repel each other, and that only when two objects of the same material are treated differently to produce charges do they attract each other. (Depending upon the treatment, two objects of the same material but treated differently may attract each other or repel each other, but two objects of the same material will never attract each other if they are treated the same way.) They should learn that negative charge is defined as the charge of a rubber rod rubbed with fur.

No attempt should be made at this level to discuss electrons or protons. Instead, students should concentrate on the basic idea of two kinds of electrical condition called plus and minus. They should learn the difference between conductors and insulators in terms of their ability to transfer charge from one object to another.

The history of electricity is a rich source from which to draw when examining various models of electricity and testing them through observation. Students should use electroscopes as a means of observing effects of charges.

Grade 10
Micro-Unit 1033. At this level, students should examine the process of induced polarization, creating their own models to account for what they observe. This provides an opportunity to postulate the existence of a negative or positive charge that moves in or on a metal-coated object to produce that polarization.

Various demonstrations or experiments involving charging conductors by induction should be carried out to give students opportunities to explain such phenomena with testable hypotheses. Students should explore the quantitative aspects of electric charge, including Coulomb's law as a proportion (not using the constant, k).

Micro-Unit 1039(a). Students should understand qualitatively the evidence leading to the Rutherford model of the atom.

Motions and Forces

ELECTRIC FORCE / COULOMB'S AND GAUSS'S LAWS, CONT.

Grade 11
Micro-Unit 1148. Students should observe the absence of electric effects inside a closed metal container as a test of the predictions of Gauss's law, which they should formulate in words. What is most remarkable is the fact that charges will distribute themselves on a metal container in such a way that the electric field everywhere inside is exactly zero. Coulombs should be used as units.

The electron should be introduced as the charged particle that moves in wires and is transferred during common electrostatic phenomena. Students should learn that ions are produced by the addition or removal of electrons from otherwise neutral atoms or molecules.

Grade 12
Micro-Unit 1252. At this level students will have acquired quantitative evidence in support of the Rutherford nuclear atom. They should now be ready to consider electricity in terms of the motion of electrons, ions, and positively charged particles. The quantized character of the basic electronic charge should be understood either through directly carrying out Millikan's experiment or having vicariously done so through reading historical material.

Elastic and Frictional Forces: Electric Forces Between Atoms and Molecules

NSES Generalization (p. 180)
Between any two charged particles, electric force is vastly greater than the gravitational force. Most observable forces such as those exerted by a coiled spring or friction may be traced to electric forces acting between atoms and molecules.

Further Description:
We can compare the relative magnitudes of electrical and gravitational forces. This can be done by using Coulomb's law and the law of universal gravitation for a pair of electrons or protons at some separation.

There are many interactions that can be reduced to electrical force upon analysis. Contact forces are the forces of repulsion of outer electrons in atoms and molecules of the interacting objects. Elastic forces involve electric forces associated with the distortion of molecules in such a way that the macroscopic effect is a force.

Elastic forces, as well as frictional forces, have associated heat transfers, so that force is not the only phenomenon involved. For most practical uses

Motions and Forces

ELASTIC AND FRICTIONAL FORCES, CONT.

involving friction in elastic systems, we need consider only the nature and magnitude of the forces involved to solve problems. Since dynamics can be approached from the point of view of either forces or energy, we may solve problems using forces and acceleration without consideration of the thermal losses associated with frictional or elastic systems. The disadvantage, however, is that one must use vectors, whereas energy is a scalar and is much easier to use in calculations.

When the energy approach is followed, thermal energy becomes a major factor limiting the law of conservation of mechanical energy and requiring the use of the first and second laws of thermodynamics. At the macroscopic level, elastic systems require consideration of Hooke's law, and frictional systems require the introduction of the coefficient of friction or viscosity in dynamics problems.

Concepts Needed:

Grade 9
Friction, fluid, viscosity, terminal velocity

Grade 10
Static friction, kinetic friction, coefficient of friction, Hooke's law, spring "constant"

Grade 11
Vector nature of frictional forces

Grade 12
Nonconservative forces

Empirical Laws or Observed Relationships:
Simple observations show that something we call friction opposes the relative motion of two surfaces in contact. The frictional force depends on the nature of the surfaces. Two kinds of friction are observed, one static and the other kinetic; heat is observed; $f < \mu N$ or $f = \mu N$ for static friction and $f = \mu N$ for kinetic friction (these relationships apply only approximately for dry friction and when the normal force is not too large); Hooke's law, $F = -kx$ for linear spring and $\tau = -k\theta$ for linear torsion.

Theories or Models:
Microscopic view of friction and relation to electrical forces; microscopic view of elastic distortion in terms of changes in separation or orientation of charges in matter

Motions and Forces

ELASTIC AND FRICTIONAL FORCES, CONT.

Learning Sequence, Grades 9–12:
Grade 9
Micro-Unit 921. Students should observe and graph the relationship between the force acting on a spring and its extension. They should recognize that the force of the spring has a direction opposite to its extension or compression.

Micro-Unit 922. Students should observe situations involving friction and deduce that when there is an applied force that produces a constant velocity but zero acceleration, there must be some additional force acting that is equal and opposite to the applied force. This is called friction. Students should also observe heat produced in frictional interactions, like rope burns, etc.

Grade 10
Micro-Unit 1018(a). Using a graph of force vs. extension of a spring students should be able to find the slope and relate it to the spring "constant" k, observing that different slopes represent springs of different stiffness.

Micro-Unit 1021(b). Students must learn that when an object is at rest (or when the force is at right angles to the motion, as in the static friction that provides centripetal force for a car going around a curve), friction is static. When the object is in motion, friction is usually kinetic. Students should solve problems involving friction on horizontal surfaces, using coefficients of friction and normal forces.

Grade 11
Micro-Unit 1120. Frictional forces in fluids should be considered, including the concept of terminal velocity. The relationship between viscosity and terminal velocity of an object moving in such a fluid can be introduced.

Grade 12
Micro-Unit 1237. Students should examine twisting of fibers or wires to note Hooke's law behavior in torsion. They should determine the "constant" k in $\tau = -k\theta$ and work problems involving friction in more complex situations, like on inclines or in fluids.

Students should develop explanations for friction and elastic systems in terms of the electrical nature of matter. An examination of SHM and the energy associated with a mass on a spring can be connected to vibrational energy modes of atoms, molecules, and crystals.

Motions and Forces

ELECTROMAGNETISM: MOVING CHARGES AND MAGNETIC FORCES

Electromagnetism: Moving Charges and Magnetic Forces

NSES Generalization (p. 180)

Electricity and magnetism are two aspects of a single electromagnetic force. Moving electric charges produce magnetic forces, and moving magnets produce electric forces. These effects help students to understand electric motors and generators.

Further Description:

The relationship between electricity and magnetism is one of the most important in all of science. The facts that a changing magnetic field can produce an electric field and a changing electric field can produce a magnetic field lead to applications involving transformers, solenoids, motors, generators, and many other devices. These phenomena are also the basis of electromagnetic waves.

Concepts Needed:

Grade 9

Magnet, magnetic pole, electromagnet, electric circuit

Grade 10

Magnetic field, electric current

Grade 11

Voltage, resistance, potential difference, parallel and series electric circuits

Grade 12

Vector fields, electromagnetic force, induced EMF, back EMF, hysteresis

Empirical Laws or Observed Relationships:

A magnetic field is created around a moving charge. The magnitude of the field depends on the magnitude of the charge, the speed of motion of the charge (the first right hand rule), and the angle between the velocity of the charge and the radius vector from the point where the field is being observed to the charge. A changing magnetic field around a conductor produces an opposing electric field in the conductor (Lenz's law, back EMF).

A force is created on a charge moving through an existing magnetic field. The magnitude of the electromagnetic force on a moving charge is proportional to the magnitude of the charge on the moving particle, the strength of the magnetic field through which it moves, the speed at which the charge is moving relative to the field, and the angle between the velocity and the field. The magnetic field around a wire carrying a current has a simple geometry, and the extension of this idea to coils of wires can be developed.

PHYSICS

Motions and Forces

ELECTROMAGNETISM: MOVING CHARGES AND MAGNETIC FORCES, CONT.

Current flow depends on voltage; flow also depends inversely on resistance. Flow divides at a junction depending inversely on the resistance along each route. Two routes (each with one unit of resistance) will be half as resistive (will allow twice the flow). Adding multiple routes (of equivalent resistance) will increase the flow proportionately.

Theories or Models:
Field theory of electricity and magnetism, electric circuits and their symbols

Learning Sequence, Grades 9–12:

Grade 9
Micro-Unit 945. Students should observe that an unmarked bar magnet suspended at its midpoint revolves to align with an approximate north-south direction, and that this is the basis for calling a pole north (seeking). They should observe properties of permanent magnets—they have poles, and like poles repel and unlike poles attract—and with iron filings and small compasses observe that we can visualize something called magnetic lines of force.

Micro-Unit 946. Students should observe that a current produces magnetism and note the direction of that magnetic field about a current-carrying wire.

Grade 10
Micro-Unit 1034(a). Students should learn to measure voltage, current, and resistance with meters. Ohm's law can be determined empirically and applied in various practical situations.

Micro-Unit 1035. Students should learn that a moving magnet produces electricity in a conductor when either the magnet or the conductor moves, but that this occurs only for certain orientations.

Grade 11
Micro-Unit 1149. Magnetic fields of solenoids can be introduced. The effects of magnetic fields on electrons can be demonstrated with television. Transformers, motors, and generators can be considered in greater quantitative detail.

Grade 12
Micro-Unit 1249. Faraday's law of induction can be developed quantitatively and used in simple problems with charged particles. The basic laws of magnetism and electricity can be formulated in equation form. These form the basis for the study of the EM spectrum.

Conservation of Energy and the Increase in Disorder (NSES, p. 180)

Work/Kinetic, Potential, and Field Energies

NSES Generalizations (p. 180)

The total energy of the universe is constant. Energy can be transferred by collisions in chemical or nuclear reactions, by light waves and other radiations, and in many other ways. However, it can never be created or destroyed. As these transfers occur, the matter involved becomes steadily less ordered.

All energy can be considered either kinetic energy, which is the energy of motion; potential energy, which depends on relative position; or energy contained by a field, such as electromagnetic waves.

Further Description:

Here work and kinetic and potential energies are considered in their different mechanical forms. Electrical energy must also be considered, and the concept of "voltage" (i.e., potential energy per unit charge) must be developed. At this point the only thing we need to do in regard to energy dissipation is to note that mechanical systems that are exchanging energy between kinetic and potential "run down." Since mass is also energy and mass energy does not conform to energy as described in the *NSES* standard, this topic needs to be developed more carefully.

The important connection between a net constant force doing work on an object and thereby increasing the velocity of the object to produce kinetic energy can be established (i.e., $F = ma$, and $W = FD = maD$. Since $v_f^2 = 2aD$, leading to $aD = v_f^2/2$, we have $W = mv_f^2/2$, which we define as *kinetic energy*). Using integral calculus, one can show that the force need not be constant and that the increase in kinetic energy as a consequence of a net force acting through some distance is exactly the increase in kinetic energy (this is called the work-energy relationship).

Conservation of Energy and the Increase in Disorder
WORK / KINETIC, POTENTIAL, AND FIELD ENERGIES, CONT.

Concepts Needed:
Grade 9:

Work, gravitational potential energy, kinetic energy

Grade 10

Simple machine, efficiency, conservation

Grade 11

Potential well, translational and rotational kinetic energy

Grade 12

Electric potential energy (and electric potential and potential difference), volt, electron volt, thermal energy, conservative force, nonconservative force, mass-energy equivalence

Empirical Laws or Observed Relationships:

In many systems, there is an interchange between kinetic and potential energies, with the total mechanical energy slowly being reduced and with an attendant increase in thermal energy of the system and its surroundings. Examples include the simple pendulum, a ball rolling back and forth in a gravitational potential well, etc.

Theories or Laws:

Law of conservation of mechanical energy; $E = mc^2$, theory of special relativity

Learning Sequence, Grades 9–12:
Grade 9

Micro-Unit 935(a). Students learn the definition of work in joules as force times the distance the object moves in the direction of the force. They should learn that the effect of a *net* force on an object is to increase its speed, and that the work done on the object by that force results only in an observable change in speed. Thus the work done produces an energy of motion we call *kinetic energy*. Work should be calculated only in situations where the force and displacement are along the same line and in the same directions.

Micro-Unit 936. At its simplest level, potential energy can be understood from the standpoint that a force working against an equal gravitational force to lift something has produced no increase in speed, but work has been done on the object by that lifting force. This energy cannot have been lost, so it is postulated to have been stored as potential energy in the system consisting of

Conservation of Energy and the Increase in Disorder
WORK / KINETIC, POTENTIAL, AND FIELD ENERGIES, CONT.

the object being lifted and the earth. Again, calculations should be simple, consisting of mgh, with units in joules.

Grade 10
Micro-Unit 1026(a). Simple machines should be understood in the context of work input equaling work output as one of the simplest applications of the law of conservation of mechanical energy. Students should then be able to solve problems involving kinetic and potential energies of simple systems and to use the law of conservation of mechanical energy to examine transformations between kinetic and potential energies for systems like a pendulum, a compressed spring, a roller coaster, or a planet in an elliptical orbit around a star.

Students should begin to see energy as an accounting system and be able to describe exchanges of mechanical energy qualitatively in "Rube Goldberg" type devices.

Grade 11
Micro-Unit 1141. At this level, students should be able to determine potential energies that change with separation, like those at great distances from a planet or the sun. They should learn force vs. distance graphs for various systems in terms of the area giving the energy (as applied, for example, to Hooke's law).

Students also should understand that the slope of a potential energy vs. distance graph gives the magnitude of the force (the actual value is the negative of the slope). They should use conservation of energy in a variety of energy transformation contexts.

Grade 12
Micro-Unit 1248. Students should be able to determine the electrical potential energy that a charge has as a consequence of another charge at some distance from the first, and the potential difference associated with that charge at two different positions in an electric field. They should learn units like volt and electron volt and be able to work with electron-volt energies.

They should be able to use the definition of work in its form that uses force and displacement vectors and to distinguish between conservative and nonconservative forces. The equivalence of mass and energy needs to be considered and used in simple calculations.

Conservation of Energy and the Increase in Disorder
HEAT, TRANSFER OF THERMAL ENERGY, SECOND LAW OF THERMODYNAMICS

Heat, Transfer of Thermal Energy, Second Law of Thermodynamics

NSES Generalization (p. 180)
Everything tends to become less organized and less orderly over time. Thus, in all energy transfers, the overall effect is that the energy is spread out uniformly. Examples are the transfer of energy from hotter to cooler objects by conduction, radiation, or convection, and the warming of our surroundings when we burn fuels.

Further Description:
This is an overgeneralization that is quite unclear. Everything does *not* tend to disorder over time. One subsystem can produce order in another subsystem over time, making the one more disordered while the other is ordered. This is what happens in photosynthesis, when glucose is synthesized (atoms made more ordered). The energy entering the system increases the order of the particles in the leaf. What is important is the overall effect.

It is the closed system, in which particles interact and into and out of which no energy or mass can enter or leave, that must become more disordered over time. This aspect of energy provides the theoretical framework to explain empirical laws of heat transfer and their connections to mechanical work done in a cycle. This leads to thermodynamic efficiency and the second law of thermodynamics. Applications include heat engines. The entropy aspects of the second law also need to be considered. The impossibility of perpetual motion machines of the first kind and especially of the second kind can now be examined.

Concepts Needed:
Grade 9
Temperature, heat, conduction, convection, radiation, insulation, phase change, gas, solid, liquid, freezing point, boiling point, calorie, calorimeter

Grade 10
Absorption, reflection, vapor, specific heat, calorimetry, mechanical equivalent of heat

Grade 11
Heat of fusion, heat of vaporization

Grade 12
Efficiency (thermodynamics), coefficient of performance, order, disorder, entropy

Conservation of Energy and the Increase in Disorder
HEAT, TRANSFER OF THERMAL ENERGY, SECOND LAW OF THERMODYNAMICS, CONT.

Empirical Laws or Observed Relationships:
Heat added = mass times specific heat times temperature change; Newton's law of cooling; Wien's displacement law; Charles' law (to establish the need for absolute temperature); absolute temperature

Theories or Models:
Stefan-Boltzmann fourth power radiation law, thermodynamics, the Carnot cycle, the entropy of systems

Learning Sequence, Grades 9–12:
Grade 9
Micro-Unit 937. At this level, students should be able to measure temperatures, know the definition of the calorie, do simple calorimetry experiments, and make other simple measurements associated with heat transfer. The concepts of radiation, convection, and conduction should be understood in qualitative ways.

Even though students will have learned the definition of work and are able to calculate work done in units of joules, they should *not* convert calories to joules at this level. (The practice of using joules for heat obscures the fundamental discoveries of the relationship between work and heat, beginning with the qualitative observations of Rumford in drilling cannon and culminating with the quantitative measurements by Joule. This fundamental and important relationship is lost from most science textbooks as a consequence of the compulsion of writers and publishers to use SI units exclusively.)

Students should understand chemical energy and changes in matter. They should be able to determine the caloric value of an energy source (like sugar).

Grade 10
Micro-Unit 1026(b). The mechanical equivalent of heat should be determined, allowing students to make the connection between calories and joules, and more importantly, between work and heat.

Grade 11
Micro-Unit 1138. At this level, students should be able to determine the latent heat of fusion of a substance, understand heats of vaporization, and determine specific heats of unknown substances through calorimetric experiments. They should observe and graph Newton's law of cooling.

Conservation of Energy and the Increase in Disorder

HEAT, TRANSFER OF THERMAL ENERGY, SECOND LAW OF THERMODYNAMICS, CONT.

Micro-Unit 1144. The basic laws of thermodynamics should be developed, along with the Carnot cycle for heat engines. Thermodynamic efficiency should be defined and determined for simple cases. The concept of entropy should be introduced and used in consideration of different systems and situations.

Grade 12
None suggested

Heat, Internal Energy, and the Kinetic Theory

NSES Generalization (p. 180)

Heat consists of random motion and the vibrations of atoms, molecules, and ions. The higher the temperature, the greater the atomic or molecular motion.

Further Description:

This *NSES* generalization confuses heat and internal energy and neglects internal potential energy as part of that energy of vibration. Heat is energy transferred to or from a system. That heat can result in changes in the internal energy of the system along with work done by the system. This latter statement is called the *first law of thermodynamics*. The heat energy (really internal energy) of a substance consists not only of the random translational and rotational motion and vibration of its atoms, molecules, and ions, but also of the internal stored potential energy associated with those atoms, molecules or ions.

This generalization is an assertion of the kinetic molecular theory. Any theory must have a set of observations and empirical laws to explain. In the case of the kinetic theory, most of that empirical basis comes from observed relationships among variables like temperature, pressure, volume, and numbers of particles for gases, and for the specific heats of gases and solids (considering vibrational modes for solids). It also comes from the experiments of Mayer and Joule that established heat as a form of energy equivalent to mechancial energy.

When a simple model of a gas is created, and Newton's laws of motion applied to particles within that model, the result indicates that the product of pressure and volume of a gas is proportional to the average translational kinetic energy of its particles. Since the empirical gas law shows that the

Conservation of Energy and the Increase in Disorder
HEAT, INTERNAL ENERGY, AND THE KINETIC THEORY, CONT.

product of pressure and volume is proportional to absolute temperature, we can conclude logically that the absolute temperature must be proportional to the average kinetic energy of particles in the gas. This is an excellent example of how a theory is created to account for certain empirical laws and observations, and how that theory leads to new information.

In this case, the theory leads to the conclusion that temperature is a measure of the average translational kinetic energy of molecules of any gas. The rotational and vibrational kinetic energies, and potential energies associated with vibration, are connected to the internal energy of that gas, but not to its temperature. Thus, oxygen gas during its phase transition from gas to liquid does not have a temperature change. This topic provides excellent examples of the history of science, coupled with the best of inquiry, leading to distinctions between empirical knowledge and the theories and models used to explain that empirical knowledge.

Concepts Needed:
Grade 9
Celsius temperature, heat, calorie

Grade 10
Pressure, volume, absolute temperature

Grade 11
Pascals, atom, molecule, mean free path, rms speed, specific heat at constant volume

Grade 12
Moles, Maxwell-Boltzmann distribution, Boltzmann's constant, momentum, impulse

Empirical Laws or Observed Relationships
Charles' law, Boyle's law, Gay-Lussac's law, specific heats of solids and gases (at constant volume)

Theories or Models:
An ideal gas as a model, kinetic-molecular theory (through an application of Newton's law to an ideal gas), the equipartition of energy theorem

Conservation of Energy and the Increase in Disorder
HEAT, INTERNAL ENERGY, AND THE KINETIC THEORY, CONT.

Learning Sequence, Grades 9–12:
Grade 9
Micro-Unit 925. This is a good opportunity to build an empirical base for subsequent theoretical work. At this level some kinetic theory can be developed descriptively and qualitatively, leading students to understand how gases exert pressures, how temperature increases change the volume or pressure of a gas under various constraints, etc. The concept of atoms and molecules can be developed as they relate to vibrations and random motion.

Grade 10
See Micro-Unit 10.22, Chemistry, p. 60.

Grade 11
Micro-Unit 1140. Newton's laws can be applied to a simple ideal gas situation to arrive at the fact that PV is proportional to the average translational kinetic energy of molecules. When the empirical law PV = nRT is then compared with this theoretical result, a conclusion is reached regarding the nature of absolute temperature: it is a measure of the average translational kinetic energy of molecules.

Grade 12
Micro-Unit 1238. Specific heats of gases and solids can be considered, leading to an understanding of equipartition of energy. High school students should not consider the anomalous effects of quantized energy states in any quantitative way at this point, but these effects should be introduced descriptively using some specific heat data contradictory to classical theory to stimulate that discussion.

Interactions of Energy and Matter (NSES, pp. 180–181)

The Wave Model: Water Waves, Seismic Waves, Sound and Light

NSES Generalization (p. 180)
Waves, including sound and seismic waves, waves on water, and light waves, have energy and can transfer energy when they interact with matter.

Further Description:
This *NSES* generalization imposes a wave model on a variety of natural phenomena. The model is successful within limits in most instances mentioned, but fails in other cases. For example, the wave model will not account for the photoelectric effect, this requiring a particle (photon model).

Feynman has successfully accounted for electromagnetic phenomena without any use of the wave model at all (R.P. Feynman, *QED: The Strange Theory of Light and Matter,* Princeton, N.J.: Princeton University Press, 1985, p. 15):

It is very important to know that light behaves like particles, especially for those of you who have gone to school, where you were probably told something about light behaving like waves. I'm telling you the way it does *behave—like particles.*

The interaction of light with matter requires the introduction of the photon, and this allows development of the quantization of energy. Oscillatory systems exhibit wave properties and are the sources of many different kinds of waves.

Concepts Needed:
   Grade 9
Period, wavelength, frequency, amplitude, transverse, longitudinal, water waves

   Grade 10
Equilibrium, medium, sound waves, seismic waves, light waves, ray, incidence, reflection, refraction, absorption, diffraction, interference

Interactions of Energy and Matter
THE WAVE MODEL: WATER WAVES, SEISMIC WAVES, SOUND AND LIGHT, CONT.

Grade 11
Resonance, phase, wave speed, intensity, index of refraction

Grade 12
Coherence, standing wave, harmonic motion

Empirical Laws or Observed Relationships:
The speed of sound in a gaseous medium depends upon properties intrinsic to the medium and the temperature of the medium. The speed of seismic waves depends upon the compressibility of the medium, the density of the medium, and whether the waves are transverse or longitudinal. The speed of surface waves on a liquid medium depends upon the compressibility and density of the medium, the depth of the medium, and the wavelength of the waves. The empirical relationship is different for a shallow medium and a deep medium; in the latter case, the dependence of speed on depth vanishes. The most precise value for the speed of all electromagnetic waves, including light waves in vacuum, is 2.99792458×10^8 m/s.

In a medium transparent to the wave, the speed is lower by an amount that depends upon the index of refraction of the medium, which in turn depends upon the frequency of the wave. The speed of a wave is related to the frequency and wavelength by the equation $v = f\lambda$.

Waves reflect off a boundary between two media at an angle that is equal to the angle of incidence; the incident ray, the normal to the boundary, and the reflected ray lie in the same plane. Reflection, under some circumstances, introduces a 180° phase shift.

When a light ray encounters a boundary between two transparent media, refraction takes place. The amount of bending of the ray is given by Snell's law, which relates the angle of incidence, angle of refraction, and the indices of refraction of both media.

The energy of a wave (the intensity of a light wave is its average energy) is proportional to the square of the amplitude. The energy (or intensity) of a wave varies with the inverse square of the distance from a point source. When waves travel through matter, there is always some absorption of the wave energy. The amount of absorption varies widely and depends upon properties of the medium and the frequency of the wave.

When waves from two or more coherent sources arrive simultaneously at the same point in space, the displacements add. Because the various waves may differ in phase, the resulting amplitudes (and therefore intensities) may

Interactions of Energy and Matter
THE WAVE MODEL: WATER WAVES, SEISMIC WAVES, SOUND AND LIGHT, CONT.

be either more or less than the arithmetic sum of the individual amplitudes, a phenomenon known as interference.

When a source of waves moves toward an observer, the observed wavelength is shorter than the emitted wavelength; also, when receding from the observer, the wavelength is longer. This is called the Doppler effect.

Theories or Models:

Waves in a material medium result from oscillations of particles of the medium. These disturbances propagate outward because every particle is linked elastically to its neighbors. Electromagnetic waves travel through a vacuum. What oscillates are electric and magnetic fields, and their propagation is governed by laws known as Maxwell's equations. These equations predict that the speed of electromagnetic waves in vacuum is determined by two constants, one that appears in Coulomb's law for electric force and another that appears in an analogous inverse square law for magnetism. This predicted speed for electromagnetic waves from the Maxwell theory matches the speed of light. Therefore, for this and other reasons we conclude that light is an electromagnetic phenomenon.

Several of the empirical laws describing electromagnetic waves, including the laws of reflection and refraction, can be derived from Maxwell's equations.

For specific wavelengths, resonance occurs on violin strings, in organ pipes, and on other structures with boundaries.

Learning Sequence, Grades 9–12:

Grade 9

Micro-Unit 919. Students should learn waves primarily in a phenomenological fashion, observing exhibits of sound waves, water waves, light waves, and waves on strings or on a slinky. They should learn what is meant by displacement, amplitude, wavelength, frequency, period, and wave speed.

Micro-Unit 950. Students should observe reflection and refraction of light and be led to discover the empirical laws governing these phenomena. They should also observe that some media are transparent to light, some media absorb light, and some partially transparent media absorb more light of some colors of the spectrum than they do of others.

Interactions of Energy and Matter
THE WAVE MODEL: WATER WAVES, SEISMIC WAVES, SOUND AND LIGHT, CONT.

Grade 10
Micro-Unit 1015(b). Students should learn that both a simple pendulum and a mass vibrating on a spring are examples of harmonic motion and that their motion can be described as similar to the motion of a particle in a medium carrying a wave. They should make the connection between periods, amplitudes, and frequencies of harmonic oscillators and the comparable wave descriptors.

Micro-Unit 1018(b). Students should develop the concept of standing waves and observe the resonance of sound waves caused by vibrating strings and air columns.

Micro-Unit 1036(a). Many students are confused between the penumbra of shadows and the phenomenon of diffraction, so it will be important for them to understand shadows and the difference between those produced by point sources and those produced by extended sources. They should learn that light exhibits diffraction and therefore has wave properties. They should observe diffraction effects, understanding that they can be constructive or destructive, and observe the Doppler effect with sound.

Grade 11
Micro-Unit 1127. Students should learn classical wave theories and determine the energy of a harmonic oscillator. They should be able to show how Snell's law is consistent with a wave theory of light and how the wave theory of light predicts the observed diffraction pattern when light passes through a grating.

Micro-Unit 1128. Students should understand how to develop and use equations to determine wavelength changes for the Doppler effect with sound.

Grade 12
Micro-Unit 1229. Students should learn the photon theory of electromagnetic radiation and understand the photoelectric effect. They should be able to connect the concept of photon emission and absorption to the concept of quantized energy levels in atoms, molecules, and nuclei.

Finally, students should understand how to develop and use the Doppler effect for light and should use it in applications associated with the movements of stars and galaxies.

Interactions of Energy and Matter
PHOTONS, ELECTROMAGNETIC WAVES, ELECTROMAGNETIC SPECTRUM

Photons, Electromagnetic Waves, Electromagnetic Spectrum

NSES Generalization (p. 180)
Electromagnetic waves result when a charged object is accelerated or decelerated. Electromagnetic waves include radio waves (the longest wavelength), microwaves, infrared radiation (radiant heat), visible light, ultraviolet radiation, X rays, and gamma rays. The energy of electromagnetic waves is carried in packets whose magnitude is inversely proportional to the wavelength.

Further Description:
This *NSES* generalization is misleading, if not erroneous. This is classical theory of electromagnetic radiation. At the atomic level, an accelerated charge in the form of an electron in an atom does not produce an electromagnetic wave. The energy "carried in packets" is not always proportional to the wavelength. Were that true, then we would encounter the contradiction of a certain wavelength of light changing its energy as it entered glass, for example, where the wavelength decreases. It is better to state that the energy is proportional to the frequency, which remains unchanged in such circumstances.

Nevertheless, classical electromagnetic wave theory is a fundamental part of physics with wide applicability. The following are important milestones in the growth of our understanding of the electromagnetic spectrum: (1) Oersted's discovery that an electric current produces a magnetic field; (2) Faraday's discovery that a changing magnetic field produces electrical effects; (3) Maxwell's synthesis and extension of earlier work in electricity and magnetism; (4) Hertz's confirmation that light is an electromagnetic phenomenon; (5) Planck's revelation that quantizing the E-M energy in a hot cavity produced agreement between theory and experiment for the blackbody radiation spectrum; (6) Bohr's theory of atomic structure explaining the line spectra emitted by gaseous atoms; (7) Einstein's use of the photon concept to explain the photoelectric effect; (8) Roentgen's discovery of X rays; and (9) Bequerel's discovery of radioactivity.

Concepts Needed:
Grade 9
Spectrum, radio waves, microwaves, infrared radiation, visible light, ultraviolet radiation, X rays

Grade 10
Visible spectrum, gamma rays

Interactions of Energy and Matter
PHOTONS, ELECTROMAGNETIC WAVES, ELECTROMAGNETIC SPECTRUM, CONT.

Grade 11
Quantum, intensity, spectral lines

Grade 12
Blackbody radiation

Empirical Laws or Observed Relationships:
Electric charges oscillating in a linear antenna at a fixed radio frequency, TV frequency, or microwave frequency emit electromagnetic waves at the same fixed frequency in all directions except parallel to the length of the antenna. The intensity is maximum in a plane perpendicular to the length of the antenna.

A hot object emits radiation that spans a range of wavelengths. The wavelength that produces the largest intensity decreases as the temperature of the body increases. An object that appears red-hot emits some energy in the red end of the visible spectrum but emits intense radiation, called infrared radiation, at somewhat longer wavelengths.

Gaseous matter that has absorbed energy from an external source spontaneously emits this energy in the form of electromagnetic radiation. Some of this radiation is at specific narrow wavelength bands in the visible and ultraviolet spectrum. The pattern of these spectral lines is characteristic of the emitting gas.

When high-energy electrons are stopped by a solid target, low-wavelength electromagnetic radiation called X-rays is emitted. The lowest wavelength in this spectrum is determined by the maximum kinetic energy of the electrons. X-rays readily penetrate nonmetallic matter but are more rapidly absorbed by dense matter, such as bone, than by less dense matter, such as muscle tissue.

Some radioactive materials spontaneously emit low-wavelength electromagnetic radiation called gamma rays. The wavelength band is narrow and characteristic of the nuclear isotope that emitted it. A gamma ray can damage a living cell that absorbs it.

Theories or Models:
Maxwell's equations predict that whenever a charge accelerates, it emits electromagnetic radiation. It is the acceleration of the charge oscillating along the length of an antenna that emits radio waves and microwaves. Electromagnetic waves transfer energy in localized packets called photons. The energy carried by each photon is proportional to the frequency of the associated wave.

Interactions of Energy and Matter

PHOTONS, ELECTROMAGNETIC WAVES, ELECTROMAGNETIC SPECTRUM, CONT.

Planck's theory of blackbody radiation pictures this radiation as emitted by electrons that oscillate because of the thermal energy contained by the hot body.

An atom that changes from one energy state to a lower one can emit a photon with an energy equal to the difference in energy between the two atomic states. When a high-speed electron is slowed or stopped, one or more photons are emitted with a total energy equal to the loss of kinetic energy experienced by the electron.

When a nucleus changes from one energy level to a lower one, a photon can be emitted with an energy equal to that lost by the nucleus. Because nuclear energy levels differ by amounts that are approximately a million times greater than the amounts between atomic energy levels, these gamma rays have wavelengths about a million times shorter than visible light.

Learning Sequence, Grades 9–12:

Grade 9

Micro-Unit 949(b). At this level, students will have observed a visible spectrum of light passed through a prism and can develop the concept of a spectrum.

Grade 10

Micro-Unit 1036(b). Students should have evidence that the entire E-M spectrum exhibits the characteristics of reflection, diffraction, interference, etc., and that radiations all along the EM spectrum travel at the same speed, c, in a vacuum.

Grade 11

Micro-Unit 1151. Students should be introduced to the connection between electricity and magnetism in terms of Ampere's law (law of Biot and Savart) and Faraday's law of induction. They should discuss examples of how E-M radiation results from accelerating charges at the level of the empirical laws described above. A demonstration where a spark gap discharge produces radio frequency emissions (detected as a burst of static on a distant AM radio) can illustrate this phenomenon.

Students should then consider blackbody radiation qualitatively, in terms of such examples as an incandescent filament in a light bulb or the red-hot embers in a wood fire.

Interactions of Energy and Matter
PHOTONS, ELECTROMAGNETIC WAVES, ELECTROMAGNETIC SPECTRUM, CONT.

Grade 12
Micro-Unit 1251. Students should make connections between Maxwell's equations and other already introduced ideas, such as E-M radiation from accelerating charges and blackbody radiation. In the case of the latter, they should note that agreement between theory and the observed spectrum requires the assumption that the energy in E-M radiation is carried in quantum packets (photons).

Quanta: The Discreteness of Atomic and Molecular Energy
NSES Generalization (p. 180-181)
Each kind of atom or molecule can gain or lose energy only in particular discrete amounts and thus can absorb and emit light only at wavelengths corresponding to these amounts. These wavelengths can be used to identify the substance.

Further Description:
This generalization has strong connections to one's understanding of *Forces and Motion* and *Conservation of Energy*. It is also related to the previous *NSES* generalization relative to electromagnetic waves.

Many interesting questions for students are raised by this generalization. How was it possible that helium was observed on the sun before it had been discovered on Earth? Scientists claim that there are organic molecules in space. How could they know? The hydrogen spectrum from very distant stars is shifted toward the red end of the spectrum due in part to the motion of the star away from Earth. How can observers on Earth be sure that they are still seeing the hydrogen spectrum?

Inasmuch as the Bohr theory contained at least one assumption that was at serious odds with accepted classical theory, why was it so readily embraced by the physicists of his era? The Bohr theory involves quantized orbits for electrons, quantized atomic energy levels, and quantized amounts of angular momentum. Are there other examples of physical quantities that are quantized?

An atom in an excited state can eventually emit a photon and drop to a lower allowed energy level. While there are theories that predict average transition rates, no theory can predict exactly when a particular atom will make the transition. What implications, if any, does this have for the philosophical view that world events are predetermined vs. the view that human free will influences the course of events?

Interactions of Energy and Matter
QUANTA: THE DISCRETENESS OF ATOMIC AND MOLECULAR ENERGY, CONT.

Students should recognize that much experimental and empirical work had been done to measure spectral wavelengths and detect patterns among them before Bohr proposed his theory. They should also understand that later developments significantly modified the Bohr theory, yet his model still has value because it is simple and concrete, in contrast to the more abstract mathematical models that have replaced it.

Concepts Needed:
Grade 9
Discrete, line spectrum, continuous spectrum

Grade 10
Emission, absorption, energy levels

Grade 11
Quantization, angular momentum, quantum number, photon

Grade 12
Vibrational modes, rotational modes

Empirical Laws or Observed Relationships:
All spectra emitted by gaseous atoms and molecules are line spectra. For example, the observed wavelengths of lines in the hydrogen spectrum, is given by the equation, $1/\lambda = (const)(1/n_1^2 - 1/n_2^2)$ (n_1 and n_2 are integers; $n_1 < n_2$). (This is Balmer's equation.)

Theories or Models:
Conservation of angular momentum.

Bohr theory of atomic structure, which includes these assumptions: the energy of the hydrogen atom is the kinetic energy of the electron plus the electrical potential energy resulting from the Coulomb force between the electron and proton; in the steady state, the electron travels in circles about the proton without radiating electromagnetic energy; and the angular momentum of the system is quantized in units of $h/2\pi$, i.e., $mvr = nh/2\pi$, where the quantum number n is 1, 2, 3 . . .

The system can change abruptly from one allowed energy level to another by emitting or absorbing a photon with whatever energy is required to conserve total energy. Atoms more complex than hydrogen ions and molecules also have quantized energy levels, although the pattern of allowed levels may be more complex than the hydrogen pattern.

Interactions of Energy and Matter
QUANTA: THE DISCRETENESS OF ATOMIC AND MOLECULAR ENERGY, CONT.

Molecules have vibrational energy and rotational energy, and each of these is separately quantized. Since the differences in energy between adjacent vibrational and rotational levels are smaller than the differences between adjacent hydrogen levels, molecular spectra lie in the infrared region of the spectrum rather than in the visible or ultraviolet region as does the hydrogen atom spectrum.

Learning Sequence, Grades 9–12:
Grade 9
Micro-Unit 949(c). Students should observe line spectra using spectrum tubes. They can also measure the wavelengths of prominent visible lines in the spectra. The important point for students is to note that the spectra are not continuous, as for a heated solid, and that no two elements appear to give the same sets of lines. They then can get at the idea of the line spectra being like the "fingerprints of the elements."

Grade 10
Micro-Unit 1039(b). At this level, students should be able to explain line spectra emitted by gaseous atoms and molecules in terms of quantization of energy.

Grade 11
Micro-Unit 1129. Have students study the pattern of measured wavelengths of the hydrogen spectrum and observe that it fits Balmer's equation (discussed above). Introduce the Bohr model for hydrogen. Discuss these assumptions as mixtures of classical ideas and remarkable creativity.

Students should examine evidence for the existence of photons, such as the photoelectric effect and Compton scattering. They should learn about quantized energy levels in atoms, molecules, and nuclei and connect the concept of a photon with quantized energy levels, using this to explain line spectra from gaseous atoms and nuclei.

Grade 12
Micro-Unit 1253. Returning to the Bohr model of the hydrogen atom, students should write equations for the total energy of the atom, the centripetal force on the electron, and the quantization of angular momentum. They should solve these equations to express the energy in terms of the quantum number n and constants such as m, e, and h. They should find the energy of the photon emitted during a transition between an energy level labeled by n_2 and a lower level labeled n_1.

Interactions of Energy and Matter

QUANTA: THE DISCRETENESS OF ATOMIC AND MOLECULAR ENERGY, CONT.

Students should be able to derive a formula for the wavelength of such radiation and show it agrees in form with the Balmer equation. Finally, have students use this theoretical equation to predict the wavelengths of a few lines in the Balmer series and compare the results with measured wavelengths.

Micro-Unit 1254. Students should consider the kinds of energy a molecule can have. They should discuss the pattern of energy levels that results from quantizing these kinds of energy independently of one another. For some simple molecules, students should compute the energy difference for adjacent levels in the vibrational levels and predict where in the spectrum a photon corresponding to that transition would fall.

Insulators, Resistors, Conductors, Semiconductors, Superconductors

NSES Generalization (p. 181)

In some materials, such as metals, electrons flow easily, whereas in insulating materials such as glass they can hardly flow at all. Semiconducting materials have intermediate behavior. At low temperatures some materials become superconductors and offer no resistance to the flow of electrons.

Further Description:

The primary connection of this generalization is to *Forces and Motion*, where the concept of electric force is first introduced. There is also a substantial connection to *Conservation of Energy*, for potential energy concepts are needed to develop the concept of electric potential.

Electric circuits involve a fairly elaborate technology that includes batteries, wires, switches, resistors, and meters. This generalization also has implications in terms of semiconducting diodes and transistors, insulators, and electroscopes.

Thompson's work with ionized matter in evacuated tubes showed a constant charge-to-mass ratio for negative ions but a charge-to-mass ratio for positive ions that varied from substance to substance. Millikan made the first successful measurement of the charge on an electron.

There were several other important events: the development in the first half of the twentieth century of a theory of solids; Shockley's invention of the transistor; Kamerlingh Onnes' discovery of superconductivity; the development of the BCS theory of superconductivity; the discovery, within the last 10 years, of high-temperature superconductors by Chu and others.

Interactions of Energy and Matter
INSULATORS, RESISTORS, CONDUCTORS, CONT.

Concepts Needed:
Grade 9
Conductor, insulator, electric current, circuits

Grade 10
Potential difference, resistance, power, metals, nonmetals, ammeter, voltmeter

Grade 11
Semiconductor, diodes, transistors, superconductor

Grade 12
Electron, charge-to-mass ratio, energy band, paired electrons

Empirical Laws or Observed Relationships:
Ohm's law (current proportional to potential for conductors), Joule's law of heating (rate of heat development in a resistor proportional to square of current)

Theories or Models:
Classical theory of resistance and current in a conductor (descriptive only); theory of energy bands in solids; ideas about what distinguishes conductors, semiconductors, and insulators (descriptive treatment only); BCS theory of paired electrons in superconductors (descriptive only)

Learning Sequence, Grades 9-12:
Grade 9
Micro-Unit 944. Let students connect series circuits that include nonmetallic elements to show that most nonmetals are insulators. They should observe that a battery normally maintains a constant potential difference that lowers only slightly when it delivers small currents. Have them observe joule heating in electrical heating elements and work done by electric motors to see that electrical energy can be converted to heat or mechanical work.

Grade 10
Micro-Unit 1034(b). With the definition of resistance as $R = V/I$, students should be able to discuss the classical theory of resistance in conductors. After measuring two or more resistances, they should show that resistance in series adds, whereas the effective resistance of resistors connected in parallel is lower than the resistance of any one resistor. They should infer the rule for calculating the effective resistance of resistors in parallel.

Interactions of Energy and Matter
INSULATORS, RESISTORS, CONDUCTORS, CONT.

Grade 11
Micro-Unit 1147. Students should define electric current as the time rate of flow of electric charge. They should be able to discuss how batteries work to move electrons from one terminal to the other and to define electric potential. Let students use different batteries, a resistor, an ammeter, and a voltmeter to discover Ohm's law. They should understand the definition of power as the rate of energy delivery. They should also carry out an investigation leading to Joule's law.

Grade 12
Micro-Unit 1250. Students should learn about the electron as a concept and describe evidence for its existence, such as the behavior of cathode rays. It would also be helpful to have a cathode-ray tube and a magnet to show that all the particles in the cathode-ray tube beam have the charge-to-mass ratio. They should be able to discuss the Millikan experiment and other evidence that charge is quantized.

Micro-Unit 1257. Students should be able to discuss the phenomenon of superconductivity, describing the BSC theory qualitatively, and to describe the advantages and disadvantages of developing and using superconducting transmission lines and magnets.

Students should be able to describe the theory of energy bands in solids and from this predict how a semiconducting transistor could behave as either a conductor or an insulator depending on how it is biased. Observing this behavior, they should discuss its various uses. Further study could be made of transistors and solid-state electronic devices. There should also be discussion of electron holes, forward bias of diodes, and LEDs.

Chemistry

NSES Topics

Structure and Properties of Matter

Chemical Reactions

Structure of Atoms

Structure and Properties of Matter

(*NSES*, pp. 178–179)

Mixtures, Elements, and Compounds: Empirical Laws and Kinetic Theory

SS&C Inferred Generalization (*NSES*, pp. 154, 178–179)

Matter, as found in nature, consists primarily of mixtures, compounds, and elements in various proportions. The observable properties of mixtures depend upon the nature of the components. A mixture can be separated into pure substances using the characteristic properties of the substances contained in the mixture.

Further Description:

This grades 5–8 generalization should have been addressed before grade 9. Many students will need to review these concepts.

Pure substances possess a set of characteristic properties, such as melting point, boiling point, density, and chemical reactivity. The properties of mixtures will vary according to the types and quantities of their components.

Mixtures can be separated into purer substances by a variety of processes, such as chromatography, distillation, and crystallization. Mixtures can be classified as either homogeneous (solutions) or heterogeneous. The relative proportions of substances in solutions can be expressed in terms of concentration (percent by mass).

Many chemical processes occur in aqueous solutions. Understanding the nature of these solutions is important for understanding biological and geochemical concepts as well as environmental issues.

Concepts Needed:

Grade 9

Matter, compound, element, mixture, melting point, boiling point, concentration, percent by mass, solutions, homogeneous, heterogeneous, qualitative, quantitative, chromatography, distillation, substance, density, characteristic property, crystallization, solubility, viscosity

Structure and Properties of Matter
MIXTURES, ELEMENTS, AND COMPOUNDS, CONT.

Grade 10
Concentration, colligative properties, concentration gradient, diffusion

Grade 11
Mole, molarity, molality

Grade 12
Vapor pressure, boiling point elevation, freezing point depression in solutions

Empirical Laws or Observed Relationships:
Law of definite proportions, law of multiple proportions

Theories or Models:
Particulate nature of matter

Learning Sequence, Grades 9–12:

Grade 9
Micro-Unit 910(a). Students should determine the mass and volume of solids, liquids, and gases and develop the concept of density as a characteristic property. They should distinguish pure substances from mixtures as matter that has a single set of characteristic properties, including boiling point, freezing point, density, solubility, viscosity, and conductivity.

Micro-Unit 928. Students should distinguish matter from energy and determine that matter, as found in nature, consists primarily of mixtures of compounds or elements.

Micro-Unit 930. Students should recognize solutions as mixtures and classify mixtures as heterogeneous or homogeneous (gas, liquid, and solid solutions). They should be able to separate mixtures into purer substances by a variety of processes, such as chromatography, distillation, and crystallization. They should observe that properties of mixtures vary with relative proportions (percent by mass) of the components.

Grade 10
Micro-Unit 1024. Students should measure properties of aqueous solutions, such as boiling point and freezing point, and deduce that they vary in a predictable way with composition and concentration. The phenomenon of diffusion should be investigated using easily distinguished solutes to establish that exchange occurs as a result of concentration gradients.

Structure and Properties of Matter
MIXTURES, ELEMENTS, AND COMPOUNDS, CONT.

Grade 11
Micro-Unit 1110. Students should determine that most substances are compounds consisting of fixed ratios of elements that are constant no matter how the compounds are found (law of definite proportions). They should also determine that in cases where a pair of elements form two or more compounds, if the mass of a given element is held constant the mass of the other element will be in simple whole-number ratios to that of the first element (law of multiple proportions).

Students should determine the empirical formulas of compounds from the known percentage compositions by mass of the elements that compose the compounds

Micro-Unit 1111(b). Students should express in terms of concentration (percent, molarity, molality) the relative proportions of substances in solutions.

Grade 12
Micro-Unit 1203. Students should determine that when pure liquids such as water are heated, the vapor pressure of the liquid increases, and that when the vapor pressure is equal to the external pressure, the liquid boils. They should determine that the boiling and freezing points of a solution depend on the molality of the solution and on the nature of the solute (ionic or covalent). They should calculate the boiling point elevations and the freezing point depressions of solutions of different molalities.

Elements, Atoms, and the Periodic Table
NSES Generalization (pp. 178–179)
An element is composed of a single type of atom. When elements are listed in order according to the number of protons (called the atomic number), repeating patterns of physical and chemical properties identify families of elements with similar properties. This "Periodic Table" is a consequence of the repeating pattern of outermost electrons and their permitted energies.

Further Description:
Elements can be grouped or classified according to their physical and chemical characteristics (metals, nonmetals, and metalloids). Early chemists

Structure and Properties of Matter

ELEMENTS, ATOMS, AND THE PERIODIC TABLE, CONT.

grouped elements with very similar properties into families. These families could be arranged into a pattern called the periodic table. Each element is composed of a single type of atom containing a specific number of protons and an equal number of electrons.

When elements are listed in ascending order of the number of protons, the periodic table is seen to be a consequence of a repeating pattern of outermost electrons. Other atomic properties also follow patterns, including atomic size, ionic size, ionization energies, electron affinity, and electronegativity. Detailed electron configurations of atoms are also reflected in the periodic table and explain variations between closely related elements.

Concepts Needed:
Grade 9
Chemical family, periodic table, metal, nonmetal, metalloid

Grade 10
Valence electron, proton, neutron, atomic number, atomic mass number, isotope

Grade 11
Atomic size, ionic size, ionization energy, electronegativity, electrode potential, isotope, periodicity

Grade 12
Energy level, sublevel, orbital electron spin, electron affinity, electron configuration

Empirical Laws or Observed Relationships:
The periodic law

Theories or Models:
Atomic theory

Learning Sequence, Grades 9–12:
Grade 9
Micro-Unit 961. Students should learn that early chemists grouped elements with similar properties into families. These families could be arranged into a pattern called the periodic table.

Students should classify or group elements according to their physical and chemical characteristics (metals, nonmetals, metalloids) and learn the names of common elements and their symbols. This should be done in conjunction with direct observation of samples of the various common elements whose

CHEMISTRY 53

Structure and Properties of Matter

ELEMENTS, ATOMS, AND THE PERIODIC TABLE, CONT.

symbols are being learned. Thus students should look at samples, touch them when safe to do so, and consider their appearance, density, and other measurable observable properties, so that the symbol for the element represents something common to their experience.

Micro-Unit 964(a). Students should develop a model to help explain observed properties of families of elements. "Black box" activities can provide experiences in constructing models and testing them.

Grade 10

Micro-Unit 1040. Students should use a model to explain the basic structure of the atom: a positively charged nucleus is surrounded by negatively charged electrons. They should then consider in more detail atomic components and the evidence for their existence and properties: the nucleus is composed of protons and neutrons (atomic mass number); in a neutral atom the number of protons in the nucleus is balanced by the number of electrons; neutrons have no charge and their number can vary in atoms of the same element (isotopes); the electrical force of attraction between a nucleus and its electrons holds the atom together.

Students should recall their ninth-grade observations of line spectra for different elements and use them as evidence for discrete energy levels in atoms.

Micro-Unit 1041. Students should understand that when elements are listed in ascending order of the number of protons (atomic number), the periodic table is seen to be a consequence of a repeating pattern of the elements' outermost electrons (valence electrons).

Grade 11

Micro-Unit 1133(b). Students should consider the Balmer, Paschen, and Lyman series in the line spectra of the hydrogen atom and show how they were used to develop a successful, but limited, atomic model.

Micro-Unit 1135. At this level, students should study the periodic table and observe that many other atomic properties follow patterns: atomic radii, ionic radii, ionization energies, electron affinity, and electronegativity.

Grade 12

Micro-Unit 1255. Students should apply quantum principles in a mechanical way to consider aspects of the refined atomic model: energy levels, sublevels, orbitals, and electron spin (electron configuration). They should

Structure and Properties of Matter

ELEMENTS, ATOMS, AND THE PERIODIC TABLE, CONT.

then relate ionization energy and electron affinity trends in the periodic table to electron configurations. This forms the theory that accounts for the historical and empirical evidence for chemical periodicity learned earlier.

Chemical Formulas and Chemical Bonds

NSES Generalizations (pp. 178–179)

Atoms interact with one another by transferring or sharing electrons that are farthest from the nucleus. These outer electrons govern the chemical properties of the element.

Bonds between atoms are created when electrons are paired up by being transferred or shared. A substance composed of a single kind of atom is called an element. The atoms may be bonded together into molecules or crystalline solids. A compound is formed when two or more kinds of atoms bind together chemically.

Further Description:

Classes of compounds formed from the transfer or sharing of outer electrons can be distinguished on the basis of solubility and electrical conductivity.

The position of elements in the periodic table and information about related trends in atomic properties can be used to predict the formulas and properties of compounds. Formulas of compounds also can be deduced from quantitative information such as percent composition and molar mass.

Lewis dot diagrams can be written to show how outermost electrons in the constituent atoms are distributed.

Concepts Needed:

Grade 9

Solubility, electrical conductivity, atomic symbols

Grade 10

Electron transfer, electron sharing, ionic bonds, covalent bonds, Lewis dot diagram, valence electrons, cations, anions

Grade 11

Molecular formula, empirical formula, percent composition

Grade 12

Bond energy, electronegativity, bond strength

Structure and Properties of Matter
CHEMICAL FORMULAS AND CHEMICAL BONDS, CONT.

Empirical Laws or Observed Relationships:
The periodic law

Theories or Models:
Lewis electron-pair bond model, the chemical bond theory

Learning Sequence, Grades 9–12:

Grade 9
Micro-Unit 963. Students should be able to interpret chemical formulas in terms of the kinds and numbers of particles (atoms) they contain. They should also be able to use ball and stick models to model a variety of structures produced by particles bonding with each other.

Grade 10
Micro-Unit 1042. Using an element's position on the periodic table and the idea of stable octets, students should determine the number of valence electrons the element would transfer or share in forming chemical bonds and the type of bonding that would occur when the element combines with another.

Micro-Unit 1043(b). Students should relate model predictions to observed properties of substances: solubility and electrical conductivity. They should use the electron pair bond concept to write Lewis dot diagrams to show how outermost electrons in constituent atoms are distributed in bonds in compounds/molecules.

Grade 11
Micro-Unit 1109. Students should determine empirical and molecular formulas of compounds from quantitative data obtained in the laboratory and information such as percent composition and molar mass from tables.

Grade 12
Micro-Unit 1219. Students should be able to relate the bonding in compounds containing ions, molecules, and networks of atoms to melting and boiling points.

Structure and Properties of Matter
MOLECULES: STRUCTURE, INTERACTIONS, AND PHYSICAL PROPERTIES

Molecules: Structure, Interactions, and Physical Properties

NSES Generalization (p. 179)
The physical properties of compounds reflect the nature of the interactions among their molecules. These interactions are determined by the structure of the molecule, including the constituent atoms and the distances and angles between them.

Further Description:
Substances can be distinguished by a wide variety of properties, such as physical state at room temperature, hardness, electrical conductivity, melting point, boiling point, solubility, malleability, ductility, and density.

The properties of compounds reflect the nature of the interactions among the molecules, atoms, or ions, which are determined by the structure of the molecules. These interactions include van der Waal's forces, dipole-dipole interactions, hydrogen bonding, and network bonding. Shapes of molecules can be predicted from the electronic structure of the atoms using Lewis dot diagrams of compounds.

Concepts Needed:
Grade 9
States of matter, electrical conductivity, melting point, boiling point, solubility, malleability, ductility, density

Grade 10
Metallic crystal, ionic crystal, covalent compound, ionic compound, chemical stability, electrostatic attraction

Grade 11
Solubility, miscibility, polarity, hydrogen bonding, network bonding

Grade 12
Van der Waal's forces, London forces, dipole-dipole interaction

Empirical Laws or Observed Relationships:
None suggested

Theories or Models:
Hydrogen bonding, network structure, electronic structure, Lewis electron-pair bond model, ionic network, intermolecular force theories (van der Waal, London, dipole-dipole)

Structure and Properties of Matter
MOLECULES: STRUCTURE, INTERACTIONS, AND PHYSICAL PROPERTIES, CONT.

Learning Sequence, Grades 9–12:

Grade 9
Micro-Unit 924. Students should be able to measure properties such as surface tension, vapor pressure, boiling and freezing points, and viscosity, and offer their own qualitative explanations of variances in these properties in terms of hypothesized intermolecular forces. They should distinguish between bonds within a molecule and interactions between molecules.

Grade 10
Micro-Unit 1043(a). Students should understand ionic bonding in terms of electron transfer and use the concept of ion charges to predict formulas for ionic compounds. They should demonstrate how ions attract ions of opposite charge from all directions and form crystal lattices.

Students should identify covalent bonding as the simultaneous electrostatic attraction of two positive ions for the valence electrons and understand that the sharing of electrons is a way of obtaining chemical stability.

Grade 11
Micro-Unit 1136. Emphasizing the relationship between molecules and structures, students should relate the properties of compounds (electrical conductivity, melting point, boiling point, malleability, ductility, and density) to the nature of the interactions among the molecules (ionic, molecular, network), which are determined by their structure.

Students should relate, descriptively and qualitatively, solubility and miscibility to the polar nature and molecular mass of the solute and solvent molecules.

Grade 12
Micro-Unit 1227. At this level, students should predict the shapes of molecules from the electronic structure of atoms using Lewis dot diagrams of compounds and use models to illustrate the structures. They should distinguish among the various types of bonds that occur between molecules and give examples of each. These include dipole moments, van der Waal's forces, and hydrogen bonds.

Giving examples, students should explain the structure of network solids as extensive networks of covalent bonds that link all the atoms in such solids.

Structure and Properties of Matter
SOLIDS, LIQUIDS, AND GASES

Solids, Liquids, and Gases: Empirical Laws and Kinetic Theory

NSES Generalization (p. 179)
Solids, liquids, and gases differ in the distances and angles between molecules or atoms and therefore the energy that binds them together. In solids the structure is nearly rigid; in liquids molecules or atoms move around each other but do not move apart; and in gases molecules or atoms move almost independently of each other and are mostly far apart.

Further Description:
The states of substances can be distinguished by differences in density and compressibility and by changes in volume as a function of temperature. For gases, quantitative empirical relationships can be established among the number of particles present, the masses of these particles, and the density and volume they occupy at standard and nonstandard conditions, thereby relating temperature, pressure, and volume.

These empirical relationships can be explained in terms of the particulate nature of matter, the forces of interaction between particles of matter, and Newton's laws of motion, leading to a connection between average kinetic energy of molecules and absolute temperature.

Concepts Needed:
Grade 9
Solid, liquid, gas, density, temperature, absolute temperature, constant pressure, volume

Grade 10
Velocity, kinetic energy, pressure, standard pressure

Grade 11
Ideal gas, compressibility

Grade 12
Particles, partial pressure, mass-volume, STP

Empirical Laws or Observed Relationships:
Boyle's law, Charles' law, Gay-Lussac's law, universal gas law, Dalton's law of partial pressures, Graham's law of diffusion

Structure and Properties of Matter

SOLIDS, LIQUIDS, AND GASES, CONT.

Theories or Models:
Kinetic molecular theory, Avogadro's hypothesis, equipartition of energy

Learning Sequence, Grades 9–12:

Grade 9
Micro-Unit 908. Students should determine the mass, volume, and density of a substance in each of its states and explain the changes using the particulate model. They should observe and contrast the physical properties of solids, liquids, and gases, and propose models that can account for the observations.

Micro-Unit 909. Students should observe phase changes in water, with measurements of mass, volume, density, and temperature.

Micro-Unit 929. Students should investigate the quantitative relationships among temperature, volume, and pressure for gases (thereby arriving at Charles' law and Boyle's law). With the Charles' law experiment, students should infer the need for an absolute temperature scale (to make the volume proportional to absolute temperature).

Grade 10
Micro-Unit 1022. Students should use the combined gas law to determine changes in volume, pressure, and temperature when two variables are held constant.

Grade 11
Micro-Unit 1113. Students should establish for gases a relationship between numbers of particles present, masses of these particles, and the density and volume occupied under standard and nonstandard conditions.

They should investigate Avogadro's hypothesis (equal volumes of gases contain equal numbers of molecules). By combining the separate gas laws, they will arrive at the universal gas law, $PV = nRT$, which they should use in various applications. They should compare the effects of changing temperature and pressure on a real sample of gas with the effects predicted by the ideal gas law.

Grade 12
Micro-Unit 1201. Explain the states of a substance in terms of the particulate nature of matter, the forces of interaction between particles, and the kinds of atoms and distances and angles between them. Also, offer an explanation in terms of kinetic theory for the empirical laws of gases.

Structure and Properties of Matter

SOLIDS, LIQUIDS, AND GASES, CONT.

Students should use Newton's laws of motion in conjunction with the ideal gas law to arrive at a quantitative relationship between average kinetic energy of molecules and absolute temperature. They should apply Dalton's law of partial pressures when investigating and applying the gas laws. They should then solve mass-volume stoichiometry problems when conditions are not at STP.

Hydrocarbons, Polymers, and Organic Macromolecules

NSES Generalization (p. 179)

Carbon atoms can bond to one another in chains, rings, and branching networks to form a variety of structures, including synthetic polymers, oils, and the large molecules essential to life.

Further Description:

Many molecules containing large numbers of atoms have useful chemical and physical properties that can be measured. Examples of physical properties are viscosity of lubricating oils; density, hardness, and melting point of plastics; and solubility of fats and oils. These properties can be explained in terms of the different bonding and structural classes of molecules and the kinds of atoms present in addition to carbon.

Concepts Needed:

Grade 9
Hydrocarbon, viscosity, density, hardness, electrical conductivity, melting point, solubility, structural formula, chains, rings, polymers, functional groups, isomers

Grade 10
Networks, branching networks

Grade 11
Alkane, alkene, alkyne, alcohol, aldehyde, ketone, ester, acid

Grade 12
Substitution reaction, elimination reaction, addition reaction, semiconductor, doping

Empirical Laws or Observed Relationships:
Polymerization

Structure and Properties of Matter

HYDROCARBONS, POLYMERS, AND ORGANIC MACROMOLECULES, CONT.

Theories or Models:
None suggested

Learning Sequence, Grades 9–12:

Grade 9
Micro-Unit 957. Students should observe the physical properties of useful organic chemicals, such as the viscosity of lubricating oils, the hardness and melting points of plastics, and the solubility of fats and oils.

Micro-Unit 965. Students should observe simple organic compounds and name and write formulas for them. It is important that experience precede terminology, and this kind of experience and naming, even without other levels of understanding, is very important.

Students should investigate the properties of (and/or synthesize when relatively simple and safe) carbon compounds useful to humans, such as dyes, medicinals, detergents, plastics, perfumes, fabrics, food, and fuels. They should also investigate the origin of these compounds (coal, petroleum, natural gas, plants, and animals).

Grade 10
Micro-Unit 1047. Students should examine the various ways that carbon atoms bond together in chains, rings, and branching networks to form a variety of structures.

Grade 11
Micro-Unit 1146. Students should draw structural formulas and name hydrocarbons that belong to the following families: alkanes, alkenes, alkynes, and aromatics. They should also draw structural formulas for isomers of various carbon compounds and for simple organic compounds containing functional groups that characterize alcohols, aldehydes, ketones, ethers, carboxylic acids, and esters.

Grade 12
Micro-Unit 1205. Students should synthesize some simple organic compounds and write balanced equations for the syntheses and for the reactions undergone by the compounds formed. They should explain and write chemical equations for polymerization reactions, selecting reactions that produce polymers that are useful in everyday life.

Chemical Reactions

(*NSES*, p. 179)

Mass and Number Conservation

NSES Generalization (p. 179)

Chemical reactions occur all around us, for example in health care, cooking, cosmetics, and automobiles. Complex chemical reactions involving carbon-based molecules take place constantly in every cell in our bodies.

Further Description:

Chemical changes can be distinguished from physical changes on the macroscopic and microscopic levels. In a chemical change one or more substances with different characteristic properties are produced. At the macroscopic level a chemical change can often be recognized by transfer of energy, changes of state (such as formation of a solid or gas), and color changes. In both chemical and physical changes, conservation of mass and energy are observed.

Chemical reactions can be represented using word equations and symbols. The coefficients of balanced formula equations represent both molecules and collections of molecules (moles). Quantitative predictions about the amounts of reactants and products can be made from information about the balanced equation when additional information such as atomic mass is available. Qualitative predictions about chemical reactivity and representation of the reactions using equations for elements in Groups IA, IIA, and VIIA can be made based on the position of these elements in the periodic table.

Concepts Needed:

Grade 9

Physical change, chemical change/reaction, word equation, chemical symbol, changes of state, states of matter, solid, liquid, gas, color, chemical formula, element, compound, atom, molecule, reactants, products, solution

Grade 10

Balanced equation

Chemical Reactions

MASS AND NUMBER CONSERVATION, CONT.

Grade 11
Mole, molar mass

Grade 12
None suggested

Empirical Laws or Observed Relationships:
Periodic law

Theories or Models:
Conservation of mass and energy, conservation of atoms in chemical reactions

Learning Sequence, Grades 9–12:

Grade 9
Micro-Unit 931. Students should observe matter undergoing change and classify the change as chemical or physical from observation of the products and the energy absorbed or released. They should infer that mass is conserved when reactions producing a gas or a precipitate are observed.

Micro-Unit 964(b). Students should use word equations to represent chemical reactions. Given balanced formula equations, they should use ball and stick models to show how atoms (but not molecules) are conserved when chemical reactions occur.

Grade 10
Micro-Unit 1028. Students should represent chemical reactions using word equations and symbols and write balanced equations to represent the reactions and illustrate the conservation of atoms.

Grade 11
Micro-Unit 1111(a). Using chemical equations and information about molar masses, students should predict the masses of reactants and products in chemical reactions. They should determine the mole and gram formula masses of familiar substances, such as salt, sugar, and butane.

Grade 12
Micro-Unit 1202. Students should qualitatively investigate gaseous diffusion testing Graham's law and understand diffusion in terms of laws of motion of particles.

Chemical Reactions

ENERGY TRANSFORMATIONS IN CHEMICAL REACTIONS

Energy Transformations in Chemical Reactions

NSES Generalization (p. 179)
Chemical reactions may release or consume energy. Some reactions such as the burning of fossil fuels release large amounts of energy by losing heat and by emitting light. Light can initiate many chemical reactions such as photosynthesis and the evolution of urban smog.

Further Description:
Chemical reactions either release or absorb energy. This is frequently evident by a change of temperature or the evolution of light. Temperature changes can be measured in the laboratory and also predicted by calculation using knowledge of specific heats and heats of reaction.

Characteristic energy changes result from reorganization of atoms in chemical reactions. Different structural arrangements of the same atoms vary in energy content. Such energy changes can be computed using thermodynamic tables.

Concepts Needed:
Grade 9
Temperature, specific heat

Grade 10
Endothermic, exothermic

Grade 11
Molecular structure, standard state, heat of reaction, entropy, enthalpy

Grade 12
Heat of formation, free energy

Empirical Laws or Observed Relationships:
Endothermic and exothermic reactions

Theories or Models:
Gibbs free energy, first and second laws of thermodynamics

Learning Sequence, Grades 9–12:
Grade 9
Micro-Unit 942. Students should observe changes in temperature or motion (an explosion) or emission of light indicating that chemical reactions either release energy (exothermic reactions) or absorb energy (endothermic reactions).

CHEMISTRY 65

Chemical Reactions

ENERGY TRANSFORMATIONS IN CHEMICAL REACTIONS, CONT.

Grade 10
Micro-Unit 1029. Students should measure the heat released or absorbed during chemical reactions in relation to the masses of the substances involved.

Grade 11
Micro-Unit 1112. Using knowledge of specific heats and heats of reaction, students should predict temperature changes in a system and compare these changes to those obtained experimentally. They should calculate the enthalpy for phase changes, based on the masses of substances used.

Students should use Hess's law to predict enthalpy changes for simple reactions. They should demonstrate that the heat associated with a reaction is dependent only on enthalpy of reactants as compared to enthalpy of final products.

Grade 12
Micro-Unit 1220. Given the mass of the reactants in a chemical reaction and a table of the heats of formation, students should predict the heat released or absorbed in the reaction. They should explain the relationship of ΔH, ΔS in predicting whether chemical reactions are spontaneous and should calculate the changes in energy for a given reaction using the Gibbs equation and appropriate tables.

Oxidation/Reduction, Acid/Base, and Radical Reactions

NSES Generalization (p. 179)
A large number of important reactions involve the transfer of either electrons (oxidation/reduction reactions) or hydrogen ions (acid/base reactions) between reacting ions, molecules, or atoms. In other reactions, chemical bonds are broken by heat or light to form very reactive radicals with electrons ready to form new bonds. Radical reactions control many processes such as the presence of ozone and greenhouse gases in the atmosphere, burning and processing of fossil fuels, the formation of polymers, and explosions.

Further Description:
Compounds can be classified according to their chemical and physical properties. They can also be classified according to their molecular structures. Some important classifications include oxidizing and reducing agents, organic and inorganic chemicals, and acids and bases. Some processes that involve

Chemical Reactions

OXIDATION/REDUCTION, ACID/BASE, AND RADICAL REACTIONS, CONT.

electron transfer include combustion, corrosion, electrochemistry, and production of metals from ores. Other reactions involve proton or hydrogen ion transfer.

The most common acid-base reaction consists of hydrogen ions combining with hydroxide ions to form water in a process called neutralization. Acid solutions can be differentiated from basic solutions by measuring their pH. In some chemical reactions under special circumstances, highly reactive species (radicals) are created and form intermediate species, such as in atmospheric chemistry and in chemical reactions occurring in flames. These species can be predicted from atomic and molecular structure and available energy.

Concepts Needed:
Grade 9
Oxidation, neutralization, acid, acid-base indicator, concentration

Grade 10
Reduction, corrosion, ion

Grade 11
Oxidizing agent, voltage (electrode potential), titration, end point, photochemistry, electroplating, electrolyze, electrolytic cell, reducing agent, half-reactions, ion, radical, pH, conjugate pairs

Grade 12
Ionization, radicals, radical reactions

Empirical Laws or Observed Relationships:
None suggested

Theories or Models:
Chemical bond, atomic structure, Bronsted-Lowry theory (definition) of acids and bases, Arrhenius's theory of ionization

Learning Sequence, Grades 9–12:
Grade 9

Micro-Unit 958. Students should define oxidation as a process in which oxygen combines with another element, distinguishing between fast oxidation as in combustion and slow oxidation as in rusting.

CHEMISTRY **67**

Chemical Reactions
OXIDATION/REDUCTION, ACID/BASE, AND RADICAL REACTIONS, CONT.

Micro-Unit 959. Students should determine an operational definition of acid and base by classifying common household substances that are acids and bases according to their chemical and physical properties. They should observe that adding a base will alter the nature of an acid solution and adding an acid will alter a basic solution.

Micro-Unit 960. Students should mix acid and base solutions back and forth to observe that one neutralizes the properties of the other. They should observe the color changes of some common indicators and note what occurs when an acid or base is added to a water solution.

Grade 10

Micro-Unit 1044. Students should identify oxygen as an element that takes electrons from fuel during combustion. They should define oxidation and reduction in terms of gain and loss of electrons and observe the oxidation of metals in various salt solutions.

Students should construct an activity table of the metals. They should test the definition of oxidation and reduction by applying the definition to reactivity of metals with salt solutions, writing equations for their observations.

Micro-Unit 1051. Students should compare the effect of incomplete oxidation of carbon to that of complete combustion and relate these to the effect on the atmosphere.

Grade 11

Micro-Unit 1155. Students should define acid and base solutions by the relative concentration of hydronium and hydroxide ions present in the solution (Bronsted acids and bases). They should use the pH scale quantitatively to determine the concentration of hydronium and hydroxide ions and investigate pH changes during titration.

Micro-Unit 1156. Students should identify oxidizing and reducing agents in redox equations and balance redox equations using half-reactions. They should examine metals and their ability to act as reducing agents in electrochemical cells. They should demonstrate the principle of the battery, and using standard reduction potential tables, predict the products of redox reactions and determine the voltage of electrochemical cells.

Chemical Reactions
OXIDATION/REDUCTION, ACID/BASE, AND RADICAL REACTIONS, CONT.

Grade 12
Micro-Unit 1226. At this level, students should interpret the meaning of ionization constants for acids in terms of acid strength, and using ionization constants calculate the concentration of the hydrogen ion in solutions. They should study how, in other reactions, chemical bonds are broken by heat or light to form very reactive radicals with electrons ready to form new bonds. Radical reactions control many processes, such as the presence of ozone and greenhouse gases in the atmosphere, burning and processing of fossil fuels, formation of polymers, and explosions.

Reaction Rates
NSES Generalization (p. 179)
Chemical reactions can take place in time periods ranging from the few femtoseconds (10^{-15} seconds) required for an atom to move a fraction of a chemical bond distance to geologic time scales of billions of years. Reaction rates depend on how often the reacting atoms and molecules encounter one another, on the temperature, and on the properties—including shape—of the reacting species.

Further Description:
Reactions are observed to take place at different rates. These rates differ according to the species present, concentration, pressure, temperature, and the presence of other substances such as catalysts. Predictions of reaction rates can be made qualitatively and quantitatively. The latter are based on the frequency and angles at which the species collide and on the energy of the collisions. Each reaction has a specific energy of activation that can be measured. Many reactions involve several steps, each of which plays an important role in determining the reaction rate.

Many reactions do not go to completion but establish an equilibrium, that is, a state in which the forward reaction and the reverse reaction have equal rates and the concentrations of the reactants and products remain constant. When changes are made to an equilibrium system (pressure, volume, temperature, concentration), predictions can be made both qualitatively and quantitatively about concentrations of the reacting species.

Concepts Needed:
Grade 9
Concentration, temperature, pressure, kinetic energy

Chemical Reactions

REACTION RATES, CONT.

Grade 10
Reaction rate, collision frequency

Grade 11
Potential energy, kinetics, activation energy, reaction mechanism, reversible reaction, equilibrium, static, dynamic, steady state, rate-determining step, activated complex

Grade 12
Reaction coordinate, equilibrium constant, mass action

Empirical Laws or Observed Relationships:
Law of mass action, Le Chatelier's principle

Theories or Models:
Chemical bond, kinetic-molecular theory, collision theory

Learning Sequence, Grades 9–12:

Grade 9
Micro-Unit 967. Students should observe several physical and chemical changes that occur at different rates and the factors that affect the rate of such changes: types of reacting substances, surface area of reactants, temperature, and concentration.

Micro-Unit 968. Using the particulate nature of matter, students should examine why temperature, concentration, and surface area are important factors in determining reaction rate.

Grade 10
Micro-Unit 1052. Students should examine quantitatively the factors (temperature, concentration and surface area) that are important in determining reaction rate. They can investigate how these factors influence very fast and very slow chemical reactions and geological processes.

Grade 11
Micro-Unit 1154. Students should contrast the nature of an equilibrium system with that of a steady-state system and relate activation energy and heat of reaction to the stability of a substance. They should hypothesize about how to shift an equilibrium and test the hypothesis using an equilibrium reaction.

Chemical Reactions

REACTION RATES, CONT.

Using Le Chatelier's principle, students should predict approximate changes in equilibrium concentrations and conditions. Using the particulate nature of matter, they should explain why changes in concentration occur in a system at equilibrium when changes in pressure are made or heat is added to or removed from the system.

Grade 12

Micro-Unit 1225. Using experimental data, students should determine the solubility product for a given solid in a water solution. They should use the solubility product and/or equilibrium constant to determine the concentration of a given species, given other pertinent data.

Using experimental data and the law of mass action, students should determine the equilibrium constant for a chemical reaction.

Catalysts and Enzymes

NSES Generalization (p. 179)

Catalysts, such as metal surfaces, accelerate chemical reactions. Chemical reactions in living systems are catalyzed by protein molecules called enzymes.

Further Description:

Catalysts can be categorized into heterogeneous (surface) and homogeneous (solutions). Comparisons can be made between these two types of catalysts regarding the way they facilitate the reorganization of atoms and molecules as the reaction proceeds. The addition of a catalyst lowers the activation energy of the forward and reverse reactions equally so that the equilibrium concentration remains unchanged.

Concepts Needed:

Grade 9

Catalyst, solution, enzymes, reaction rate

Grade 10

None suggested

Grade 11

Activation energy, reaction coordinate, equilibrium, adsorption, reversible reaction

CHEMISTRY 71

Chemical Reactions

CATALYSTS AND ENZYMES, CONT.

Grade 12
Homogeneous catalyst, heterogeneous

Empirical Laws or Observed Relationships:
Catalysis

Theories or Models:
Chemical bonds, catalytic theory

Learning Sequence, Grades 9–12:

Grade 9
Micro-Unit 969. Students should observe the decomposition of hydrogen peroxide. Adding manganese dioxide, they should observe the rapid evolution of a gas. They should also observe other examples of catalysts and their effects on chemical reactions, including the action of yeast in fermentation as an example of the action of an enzyme.

Grade 10
None suggested

Grade 11
None suggested

Grade 12
Micro-Unit 1221. At this level, students should use equations to show how homogeneous catalysts form intermediate reactions in the process of speeding up the overall reaction. They should calculate enthalpy changes for catalyzed and uncatalyzed reactions to show that the enthalpy change is constant and determine the effect of a catalyst on reversible reactions—activation energies of forward and reverse reactions.

Students should compare and interpret coordinate plots and energy probability plots for catalyzed and noncatalyzed reactions.

Micro-Unit 1222. Students should identify enzymes other than yeast that are involved in reactions in cells. They should measure and compare quantitative changes in rates vs. mass of catalyst added. They should observe the action of homogeneous catalysts (present in the same phases as the reactants) and heterogeneous catalysts (reactants are in a different phase) and describe the difference between them in terms of phases of the involved species and the way the catalysts work on the molecular level.

Structure of Atoms
(*NSES*, p. 178)

The Nuclear Atom and Its Components: Electrons, Protons, and Neutrons

NSES Generalization (p. 178)
Matter is made of minute particles called atoms, and atoms are composed of even smaller components. These components have measurable properties, such as mass and electrical charge. Each atom has a positively charged nucleus surrounded by negatively charged electrons. The electric force between the nucleus and electrons holds the atom together.

Further Description:
Convincing evidence exists today that matter is composed of minute particles called atoms. Experiments can be done with cathode-ray tubes, electroscopes, and radioactive isotopes to show that matter has small positively and negatively charged components. Each of these components has a measurable amount of mass and, except for the neutron, electrical charge.

More detailed experimental analyses by Thomson, Rutherford, Millikan, Bohr, Sommerfeld, Pauli, Hund, and many others have led to the creation of an atomic model consisting of a small positively charged nucleus surrounded by negatively charged electrons. The electrons occupy most of the space in the atom and are held to the nucleus by electrical forces of attraction.

Each electron in an atom has its own distinct amount of energy. In flames, electrons in atoms can gain enough energy to make transitions to higher energy levels. When they move back to their original levels, light is emitted having specific energies (corresponding to the specific wavelengths of light observed), in many cases giving an intense color to the flame.

Such observations led to a suggested model of the atom in which electrons have discrete amounts of energy. Quantitative aspects of this model work well for atoms with single outer electrons. However, observations of spectra of atoms with multiple outer electrons, and consideration of the wave properties of electrons, led to development of a wave-mechanical model for the electrons in atoms, with each electron in a stationary wave pattern called an orbital.

Structure of Atoms

THE NUCLEAR ATOM AND ITS COMPONENTS, CONT.

Concepts Needed:
Grade 9
Atom, electrical charge, spectrum, electroscope, proton, electron, nucleus

Grade 10
Cathode

Grade 11
Electron, energy level, orbital, radioactive isotopes, nucleus

Grade 12
Particle, wavelength uncertainty, quanta

Empirical Laws or Observed Relationships:
Emission line spectra for elements, Hund's rule

Theories or Models:
Atomic theory, wave-mechanical model, Thomson model, Rutherford model, Bohr model, Sommerfeld model, Pauli exclusion principle, Heisenberg uncertainty principle, Planck's theory, de Broglie relation

Learning Sequence, Grades 9–12:
Grade 9
Micro-Unit 943(a). Students should observe direct electrical properties of matter, such as static electricity and conductivity.

Micro-Unit 949(a). Students should observe the visible spectra of light emitted from heated elements and compounds and interpret the differences in terms of the different electronic structures of atoms and molecules. They should distinguish between continuous, band, and line spectra.

Micro-Unit 962. Students should relate electrical properties of matter in a qualitative way to an atomic model. They should compare J. J. Thomson's model of the atom to that subsequently proposed by Rutherford and examine the evidence that led to rejection of the Thomson model and acceptance of the Rutherford nuclear model: the atom consists of a nucleus containing most of the mass and with a positive charge, around which move enough electrons to make the atom electrically neutral.

Grade 10
Micro-Unit 1038. Students should observe conductivity of electricity in gases and the behavior of electrons in cathode-ray tubes as they pass through magnetic and electrical fields and relate these observations to J. J. Thomson's discovery of the electron.

Structure of Atoms

THE NUCLEAR ATOM AND ITS COMPONENTS, CONT.

Grade 11

Micro-Unit 1133(a). Students should review the historical development of atomic structure. Bohr's model worked well quantitatively for atoms with single electrons. They should describe the difficulties in fitting this theory to observations of spectra of atoms with multiple electrons, and how that led to the development of a wave-mechanical model for the electrons in atoms.

Grade 12

Micro-Unit 1256. Students should apply the de Broglie relation—a particle of mass, m, and speed, v, postulated to have an associated wavelength, h/mv—and describe the evidence for the wave properties of the electron (Davisson-Germer experiment). This could include a discussion of the electron microscope and why its resolution exceeds to such a great degree that of an optical microscope.

Students should discuss Heisenberg's uncertainty principle—it is impossible to know simultaneously both the momentum and position of an electron. They should show that they understand how Planck had to fit an empirical formula with quanta of energy to describe the continuous distribution of light emitted by a hot solid at different temperatures (he had to assume that atoms of solids vibrate with a distribution of frequencies, but for each oscillator the possible energies are proportional to integer multiples of the frequency).

Students should apply Hund's rule in determining the arrangement of electrons within a subshell. They should apply the Pauli exclusion principle—no two electrons in an atom can have the same set of four quantum numbers (n, l, m_l, and m_s)—to electrons in atoms in terms of energy levels (1, 2, 3, . . .), sublevels (s, p, d, f), orbitals, and electron spin.

Protons, Neutrons, and Isotopes

NSES Generalization (p. 178)

The atom's nucleus is composed of protons and neutrons, which are much more massive than electrons. When an element has atoms that differ in the number of neutrons, these atoms are called different isotopes of the element.

Further Description

Early chemists, such as Richards, determined the relative masses of atoms by careful comparison of masses of various compounds made from a succession

Structure of Atoms

PROTONS, NEUTRONS, AND ISOTOPES, CONT.

of similar elements. The development of the periodic table was assisted by placing the elements in ascending order of these masses. The discovery of neutrons, and the recognition that atomic masses did not fit exactly in ascending order in the proposed form of the periodic table, led to the proposal that the atomic nucleus contains uncharged neutrons as well as positively charged protons.

Atoms of the same element that have different numbers of neutrons are called isotopes of the element. Chemical properties are related predominantly to the number of protons and not to the number of neutrons present in the nucleus. Yet, very small variations in the chemical behavior of isotopes are used as diagnostic tools in understanding slow geochemical processes. These variations can be used, for example, to track paleoclimatic changes.

The atomic mass of an element is a weighted average of the atomic masses of the isotopes of the atom found in nature. The masses of the individual isotopic atoms are measured in a mass spectrometer by precise comparison to the mass of a carbon atom containing six protons and six neutrons. Since the mass of one mole of such carbon atoms is defined by international agreement as 12.0000 grams, the molar masses of any other elements can be established. The mass of a nucleus is not exactly equal to the sum of the masses of the neutrons and protons because some of this mass has been converted to energy as the nucleus formed (binding energy).

Concepts Needed:

Grade 9
None suggested

Grade 10
Nucleus, neutron, proton, atomic mass, atomic mass number, isotope

Grade 11
X-rays, wave lengths, atomic number, periodicity

Grade 12
Nucleus, neutron, proton, atomic mass, isotope, mole, atomic number, molar mass, mass defect, binding energy

Empirical Laws or Observed Relationships:
Conservation of mass-energy, periodic law

Structure of Atoms

PROTONS, NEUTRONS, AND ISOTOPES, CONT.

Theories or Models:
The Rutherford nuclear atom

Learning Sequence, Grades 9–12:

Grade 9
None suggested

Grade 10
Micro-Unit 1056. Students should understand that atoms of a given element consist of several types (isotopes) that differ from one another in mass number (same atomic numbers but different mass numbers attributed to a different number of neutrons, from mass spectrometry). They should explore how isotopes are used as diagnostic tools in understanding geochemical processes and tracking paleoclimatic changes.

Grade 11
Micro-Unit 1134. Students should examine the work of Moseley, who, using X-rays, found a mathematical relationship between the wavelengths of the X-rays produced and the atomic numbers of the elements used as targets. This resulted in the redefinition of the periodic law.

Grade 12
Micro-Unit 1246. Students should understand that atomic mass is the weighted average of the atomic masses of naturally occurring isotopes converted to atomic mass units. They should use the definition that an atomic mass unit equals identically one-twelfth the mass of a carbon-12 atom.

Students should define the binding energy of a nucleus as the energy needed to break a nucleus into its individual protons and neutrons. They should then calculate the mass defect of a nucleus, which equals the total mass of its individual nucleons taken as separate particles, minus the mass of the nucleus.

Finally, students should apply the law of conservation of mass and energy, $E = mc^2$.

Structure of Atoms
NUCLEAR FISSION AND FUSION

Nuclear Fission and Fusion
NSES Generalization (p. 178)

The nuclear forces that hold the nucleus of an atom together, at nuclear distances, are usually stronger than the electric forces that would make it fly apart. Nuclear reactions convert a fraction of the mass of interacting particles into energy, and they can release much greater amounts of energy than atomic interactions. Fission is the splitting of a large nucleus into smaller pieces. Fusion is the joining of two nuclei at extremely high temperature and pressure, and is the process responsible for the energy of the sun and other stars.

Further Description:
In chemical changes atoms are rearranged into different configurations. In nuclear changes particles in atomic nuclei are either increased in number, decreased in number, or transformed one into another. The energy changes involved in these processes are many orders of magnitude larger than those in chemical changes. This is because the nuclear forces between the nuclear particles in the nucleus are much stronger than the electrical forces that hold atoms together.

Important nuclear reactions are fission, fusion, and radioactive decay. In fission a very large nucleus splits into two large and approximately equal fragments with release of a large amount of energy, mostly kinetic. Fusion occurs when small nuclei collide with sufficient energy to overcome the repulsion between them from their positive charges.

In the sun and other stars, the energy for successful collision comes from neighboring fusion reactions, which, when they occur, release large amounts of energy, raising the sun's temperature to a very high level. Fusion reactions are employed to create new (superheavy) elements and are prospective energy sources for electric power production.

Neutrons and protons are thought to consist of smaller particles called quarks. The properties of quarks are still the subject of much research.

Concepts Needed:
Grade 9
Chain reaction

Grade 10
Nuclear reaction, fission, fusion, isotopes, positive charge, mutual repulsion, nucleon force barrier.

Structure of Atoms

NUCLEAR FISSION AND FUSION, CONT.

Grade 11
Nuclear force, nuclear reaction, exothermic reactions, kinetic energy, coulomb force barrier

Grade 12
Nuclear stability, nucleons, quarks

Empirical Laws or Observed Relationships:
Radioactivity, conversion of matter and energy

Theories or Models:
Mass-energy relationship, $E = mc^2$, nuclear transformations, quark model, theories of nuclear stability

Learning Sequence, Grades 9–12:

Grade 9
Micro-Unit 966(c). Students should create and examine macroscopic analogs to chain reactions, like mousetrap/Ping Pong™ ball arrangements, to gain the concept of a chain reaction.

Grade 10
Micro-Unit 1059. Students should examine the general principle of a chain reaction and qualitatively discuss chain reactions of fusion and fission. They should balance nuclear reaction equations for fusion and fission given information on typical reactants and products. They should be able to explain these processes in terms of when fission occurs (when a large nucleus splits into two large and approximately equal fragments with release of a large amount of energy, mostly kinetic) or when fusion occurs (when small nuclei collide with sufficient energy to overcome the repulsion between them as a result of their positive charges).

Students should compare the benefits and hazards of nuclear fission and fusion reactors as energy sources.

Grade 11
Micro-Unit 1161. Students should examine the rearrangement of electrons into different configurations in chemical changes, where the nuclei of atoms are not affected. They should also consider nuclear transformations, where particles in atoms are either increased, decreased, or transformed one into another.

Students should contrast the relative magnitudes of energy associated with nuclear fission of U-235 to energies associated with chemical changes and compare mass changes for the two processes. They should note that energy

Structure of Atoms

NUCLEAR FISSION AND FUSION, CONT.

changes involved in fission (and fusion) processes are many orders of magnitude larger than in chemical changes because the nuclear forces between the nuclear particles are much stronger than the electrical forces that hold atoms together.

Grade 12

Micro-Unit 1247. Students should relate nuclear reactions to processes that occur naturally in the sun and other stars, where energy for successful fusion comes from neighboring fusion reactions. These reactions, when they occur, release large amounts of energy, raising the sun's temperature to a very high level.

Students should understand how fission and fusion reactions are used to create new elements or useful isotopes and are prospective energy sources for electric power production. These reactions should be compared to chemical sources of electrical power. Finally, students should study subatomic particles, such as hadrons, leptons, and quarks, and their implications for the ultimate structure of matter.

Radioactivity and Its Applications

NSES Generalization (p. 178)

Radioactive isotopes are unstable and undergo spontaneous nuclear reactions, emitting particles and/or wavelike radiation. The decay of any one nucleus cannot be predicted, but a large group of identical nuclei decay at a predictable rate. This predictability can be used to estimate the age of materials that contain radioactive isotopes.

Further Description:

The isotopes of some elements are unstable. These isotopes undergo spontaneous nuclear decay reactions and emit particles and/or electromagnetic radiation. The decay of a large number of atoms of a specific isotope occurs at a predictable rate, and the isotope is identified as having a characteristic half-life.

Useful applications of radioactive decay can be found in medical diagnosis and therapy, in food preservation, and in estimating the age of materials containing specific radioactive isotopes. Radiation emitted in decay can consist of helium-4 nuclei (alpha radiation), positive or negative electrons (beta decay), or electromagnetic radiation (gamma radiation). In beta decay, neutrinos are also emitted.

Concepts Needed:
Grade 9
Half-life

Structure of Atoms

RADIOACTIVITY AND ITS APPLICATIONS, CONT.

Grade 10
Isotope, electromagnetic radiation, radioactive decay, neutrino, beta decay, transmutation, transuranium elements

Grade 11
Radioactive isotopes, stable nucleus

Grade 12
None suggested

Empirical Laws or Observed Relationships:
Alpha-beta-gamma radiations, spontaneous nuclear reactions, conservation of mass-energy

Theories or Models:
Law of radioactive decay, theories of nuclear stability

Learning Sequence, Grades 9–12:

Grade 9
Micro-Unit 966(a). Students should develop an understanding of average lifetime for a radioactive material expressed in terms of half-life ($1.433T_{1/2}$). They should use the results of such calculations for various radioactive materials to consider implications for radioactive wastes.

Grade 10
Micro-Unit 1057. Working with typical counting data from real radioactive sources, students should construct graphs and determine the half-life of a source. They should distinguish among the various types of radioactive decay—alpha, beta, and gamma, positron, and electron capture—and they should be able to write equations representing these types.

Grade 11
Micro-Unit 1104. Students should trace changes in radioactive elements as they decay until a stable nucleus is reached, and estimate the age of a given sample of carbon-containing organic material from mass data and activity. Finally, they should describe applications of radioactive isotopes in chemical analysis, medical therapy, and diagnosis.

Grade 12
None suggested

Biology

NSES Topics

The Cell

Matter, Energy, and Organization
in Living Systems

The Molecular Basis of Heredity

Biological Evolution

The Interdependence of Organisms

The Cell

(*NSES*, pp. 184–185)

Cell Structures That Underlie Cell Functions

NSES Generalization (p. 185)

Cells have particular structures that underlie their functions. Every cell is surrounded by a membrane that separates it from the outside world. Inside the cell is a concentrated mixture of thousands of different molecules which form a variety of specialized structures that carry out such cell functions as energy production, transport of molecules, waste disposal, synthesis of new molecules, and the storage of genetic material.

Further Description:

The fundamental unit of all organisms is the cell. By the early 1800s it had been determined that all organisms are made up of cells and that the cells carry on the processes characteristic of all living organisms. The complexity of cell structure and function has been made evident with advances in technology. Through the development of optical and electron microscopes and breakthroughs in molecular biology, much information has been discovered concerning the structure and function of cells.

The cell membrane transports protein-regulated substances entering the cell. Regardless of the type of cell, all cells carry out basic activities of life maintenance: absorption and conversion of energy, digestion, biosynthesis, respiration, excretion, secretion, generation of a membrane potential or voltage, response, and reproduction. These activities are maintained by the interaction of specialized structures in the cell called organelles. The transport proteins in the cell membrane, also found in membranes of cell organelles, are highly selective. They can move substances counter to diffusion. Transport proteins that move substances against diffusion gradients require energy, and substances are said to be actively transported into or out of the cell. This regulation of exchanges of substances into and out of a cell is essential to cell maintenance.

Of specific importance in maintaining homeostasis in cells are cell membranes. The cell membrane controls what enters and leaves the cell. This

The Cell

CELL STRUCTURES THAT UNDERLIE CELL FUNCTIONS, CONT.

selective permeability depends upon the structural components making up the membrane. These structural components enable cell membranes to identify specific substances the cell needs and to transport them into the cell. In addition, the cell membrane sometimes prevents harmful substances or substances that the cell does not need from entering the cell.

Within the cell exist several "organelles." Organelles are specialized bodies that serve specific life functions of the cell. The organelle that is critical to fully functioning cells is the nucleus. The nucleus contains chromatin, a complex of DNA and proteins necessary for storage and transport of genetic information. Besides the nucleus, there are several other important organelles necessary for cell maintenance, such as the mitochondria, which convert sugar into energy for the cell; ribosomes, which manufacture enzymes, hormones, and structural proteins of the cell; and the Golgi body, which synthesizes carbohydrates and chemically tags proteins for distribution in the cell.

Some organelles are specific to plant cells, for example the plastids. The most important plastid found in plants is the chloroplast, which manufactures glucose by using light energy to split water molecules. Other plastids, such as leucoplasts, serve as storage locations for starch and oil. Microtubules and actinfilaments are components of a complex network of protein filaments called the cytoskeleton. The cytoskeleton maintains the shape of the cell, allows the cell to move, and gives it the ability to provide and maintain directed pathways from one part of the cell to another for its organelles.

Evolutionary aspects of parts of the cell must be considered if structure and function are to be understood. Some organelles such as the mitochondria and chloroplasts are thought to have originally existed as separate bacteria cells. During evolutionary stages these cells were engulfed by large prokaryotic cells, but they still maintained some autonomy.

Concepts Needed:

Grade 9
Microscopy, absorption, nutrition, excretion, secretion, cell membrane

Grade 10
Permeability, diffusion, osmosis, concentration gradients, cell size, toxicity, surface-to-volume ratio

Grade 11
Prokaryote, eukaryote, transport proteins, active transport

Grade 12
Polarity, membrane selectivity, membrane potential

The Cell

CELL STRUCTURES THAT UNDERLIE CELL FUNCTIONS, CONT.

Empirical Laws or Observed Relationships:
Only cells beget cells, phenomenon of membrane potential, osmosis, the process of diffusion, the process of active transport, surface-to-volume ratio as a limiting factor

Theories or Models:
Fluid mosaic model, complementarity of structure and function, the cell as the functional unit of life, all organisms are made of cells of various kinds (cell theory), active transport

Learning Sequence, Grades 9–12:

Grade 9

Micro-Unit 932 Students should understand how we know that cells are the fundamental unit of all organisms. They should examine how plant and animal cells are different.

Micro-Unit 933. Students should examine the distinctions among the most important organelles—nucleus, ribosome, mitochondrion, and chloroplast—and study the cell concept, comparing cell functions with human biological functions. They should be able to describe the chloroplasts of plant cells.

Grade 10

Micro-Unit 1025. Students should investigate diffusion and osmosis as important processes in cell maintenance and distinguish between hypotonic, hypertonic, and isotonic solutions. They should understand that a membrane is a boundary and relate the structure of the cell membrane to the observed processes of diffusion and osmosis.

Students should understand how cell size and cell shape are related to surface-to-volume ratio and how that ratio limits cell size and function.

Micro-Unit 1054. Students should examine and compare the organelles of the cell needed for secretion, digestion, synthesis, storage, and cell movement.

Grade 11

Micro-Unit 1159. Students should compare facilitative transport with active transport, describing the sodium-potassium pump process as an active transport system.

The Cell
CELL STRUCTURES THAT UNDERLIE CELL FUNCTIONS, CONT.

Grade 12
Micro-Unit 1228. Students should understand the importance of polarity and selectivity of the cell membrane and the evolutionary significance of membranes in the origins of the first cells. They should study how parts of the cell have evolved and how that evolution relates to structure and function of the various cell components.

Cell Chemistry: Metabolism, Catalysts, and Photosynthesis

NSES Generalizations (p. 184)
Most cell functions involve chemical reactions. Food molecules taken into cells react to provide the chemical constituents needed to synthesize other molecules. Both breakdown and synthesis are made possible by a large set of protein catalysts, called enzymes. The breakdown of some of the food molecules enables the cell to store energy in specific chemicals that are used to carry out the many functions of the cell.

Plant cells contain chloroplasts, the site of photosynthesis. Plants and many microorganisms use solar energy to combine molecules of carbon dioxide and water into complex, energy rich organic compounds and release oxygen to the environment. This process of photosynthesis provides a vital connection between the sun and the energy needs of living systems.

Further Description:
Metabolism, which is defined as the sum of all chemical reactions occurring in a cell, involves the activities of enzymes. Enzymes are large protein molecules that serve as catalysts to lower the energy required for reactions to take place in cells. Enzymes as catalysts also function in speeding up rates of reactions. Because of enzymes, cell metabolism is carried out with greater speed and at lower temperatures than would otherwise be required. Therefore, the breakdown and synthesis of materials in a cell is more efficient.

Cells can manufacture thousands of enzymes. However, cells will only produce enzymes needed for specific reactions. Therefore, not all cells carry all the same enzymes.

Because of the catalytic activities of enzymes, complex chemical processes like the conversion of sugar to release energy can take place. This energy is stored in the bonds of a chemical molecule called ATP. ATP is used for all chemical reactions requiring energy. In cells some of the most important

The Cell

CELL CHEMISTRY: METABOLISM, CATALYSTS, AND PHOTOSYNTHESIS, CONT.

reactions requiring energy are active transport, protein synthesis, DNA synthesis, and cell division.

Considered to be the most important chemical reaction on this planet, photosynthesis is a process that converts the physical energy of light into the chemical energy of ATP and sugar in the form of glucose. Not only do plants undergo photosynthesis, but also some protists (e.g., algae) and some bacteria (e.g., purple sulfur bacteria). Over the history of Earth, the photosynthesis of first bacteria and then algae is largely responsible for Earth's level of oxygen concentration, which occurred over a period of 1.5 billion years before green plants began to appear.

Glucose, a sugar, is the fundamental energy material of the food chain. In plant and animal cell respiration, mitochondria use glucose to make ATP. Photosynthesis as a process is restricted to plants and a few specialized bacteria and protists. Chloroplasts are the "factories" of carbohydrate production in plants. Chloroplasts are organelles that contain the necessary pigments, named chlorophyll, that will capture light energy. Along with chlorophyll, the chloroplast contains other important chemical compounds, such as enzymes, that are necessary for the synthesis of glucose.

The overall process of photosynthesis requires light, chlorophyll, CO_2, and water as basic raw materials to produce glucose. Through a series of complex chemical pathways involving light and dark reactions and two photosystems, I and II, ATP and carbohydrates are synthesized.

Concepts Needed:
Grade 9
Energy, matter, chemical reaction, synthesis, metabolism, energy bonds, enzymes, pigments, carbohydrates

Grade 10
Energy of activation, enzyme action

Grade 11
Anabolism, catabolism, catalyst cofactors in enzyme, allosteric effect, competitive inhibition, feedback mechanisms, ATP synthesis

Grade 12
Grana, stoma, ATP action spectrum, chlorophyll, light, wavelengths

Empirical Laws or Observed Relationships:
The process of photosynthesis, the light and dark reactions, photolysis of water, Calvin-Benson C_3 and C_4 pathways

The Cell

CELL CHEMISTRY: METABOLISM, CATALYSTS, AND PHOTOSYNTHESIS, CONT.

Theories or Models:
Enzyme substrate complex, enzyme specificity, induced-fit hypothesis, photosystems I and II, CO_2 fixation, bond energy, cyclic photophosphorylation, chemiosmosis, photolysis, clock reactions

Learning Sequence, Grades 9–12:

Grade 9
Micro-Unit 934(a). Students should observe chloroplasts of plant cells, the site of photosynthesis. They should investigate how cells in green plants trap sunlight and convert light energy into the chemical-bond energy of sugar, giving off oxygen as a by-product. The energy in sugar then becomes available for use by plants and all other living organisms.

Grade 10
Micro-Unit 1053. Students should understand what catalysts are and compare nonbiological catalysts to biological catalysts like enzymes. They should observe fundamental aspects of cellular enzyme activity and explore factors, such as pH and temperature, that affect reaction rates.

Grade 11
Micro-Unit 1158. Students should understand how energy is transformed to sugar in the carbon cycle through photosynthesis and examine the fine structure of chloroplasts.

They should study the C_3 pathways in photosynthesis, photosystems I and II, and CO_2 fixation, and compare the C_3 pathway with the C_4 pathway for certain plants, noting the evolutionary importance of C_4 plants. They should identify factors that influence rates of photosynthesis, such as pollutants and increases in CO_2 levels in the atmosphere.

Grade 12
Micro-Unit 1223. Students should distinguish the basic components of plant metabolism, which involves the breaking down and synthesis of complex organic compounds from inorganic compounds. They should examine the *induced-fit* model of enzyme function and the catalytic cycle of an enzyme.

Students should investigate the effects of pH and temperature on enzymes and how enzymes are controlled by allosteric interactions. They should distinguish between competitive and noncompetitive inhibition. They should also understand the importance of cofactors and co-enzymes in relation to vitamins in human diets and how metabolic pathways are regulated.

BIOLOGY

The Cell

DNA, RNA, AND GENETIC ENGINEERING

DNA, RNA, and Genetic Engineering

NSES Generalizations (pp. 184–185)

Cells store and use information to guide their functions. The genetic information stored in DNA is used to direct the synthesis of the thousands of proteins that each cell requires.

Cells can differentiate, and complex multicellular organisms are formed as a highly organized arrangement of differentiated cells. In the development of these multicellular organisms, the progeny from a single cell form an embryo in which the cells multiply and differentiate to form the many specialized cells, tissues and organs that comprise the final organism. This differentiation is regulated through the expression of different genes.

Cell functions are regulated. Regulation of cells occurs both through changes in the activity of the functions performed by proteins and through the selective expression of individual genes. This regulation allows cells to respond to their environment and to control and coordinate cell growth and division.

Further Description:

The language of life is based upon the chemical composition of DNA. This macromolecule spells out codes that dictate messages which are translated by cells into the traits of organisms. Messages are in the form of RNA, a single-stranded nucleic acid. RNA carries the messages in the form of triplet-sequence codons. These sequences are composed of specific chemical molecules called nitrogenous bases—adenine, guanine, cytosine, and uracil. The arrangement of these bases into triple combinations results in the production of 64 possible codons. These sequences of three bases correspond to specific amino acids. Amino acids are the building blocks of proteins, and proteins are expressed as traits. In the cell the process of building proteins is controlled by DNA, which is transcribed to form RNA, which in turn is translated to form proteins. All organisms are made up of thousands of characteristics or traits coded for by DNA.

Control of cellular function is generated by genetic components within the nucleus of each cell. This control is indirect: the nucleus sends messages into the cytoplasm where they are translated into proteins. Proteins then perform thousands of chemical reactions in the cell.

The production of all proteins is regulated by the nucleus of each cell. It is believed that a gene regulatory system in the nucleus can "switch on" or

The Cell

DNA, RNA, AND GENETIC ENGINEERING, CONT.

"switch off" protein production; therefore, only essential proteins will be produced for needed activities of the cell.

Development is the process whereby a fertilized egg divides and differentiates into tissues, organs, organ systems, and ultimately the organism. The process of development is different in animals and plants. In animals the development of the embryo can be divided into the following stages: cleavage, germ layer formation, and organ development. By the action of cell division the fertilized egg will divide into masses of cells that will then develop into discrete germ layers. Germ layers will further develop into specific organs and organ systems. This complex process is under the control of gene mechanisms of the female parent as well as those of the developing embryo.

In higher plants the differentiation of the zygote is activated by hormones produced in the embryo. Through cell division embryonic regions will form the first root, stem, and leaf structures. Upon germination the embryo will again begin to divide and differentiate into a seedling.

Concepts Needed:

Grade 9
Growth, mitosis

Grade 10
Codes, characteristics, traits, nucleus, mitosis

Grade 11
Replication, double helix, DNA, codon, polymer, translation, transcription, nitrogen bases, triplets, templates, proteins, amino acids, RNA, protein synthesis

Grade 12
Intron, exon, permease, operator gene, regulation gene, repressor protein, inducer substance, structural gene, differentiation, fertilization, germ layers

Empirical Laws or Observed Relationships:
The genetic code, base pair complementarity, feedback mechanisms, the process of developmental onset, semiconservative replication, chronologically triggered development, embryo germ layer processes, organogenesis

Theories or Models:
One gene-one enzyme theory, gene theory, operon theory, genetic control of cell processes

The Cell

DNA, RNA, AND GENETIC ENGINEERING, CONT.

Learning Sequence, Grades 9–12:

Grade 9
None suggested.

Grade 10
Micro-Unit 1050. Students should understand the universality of the DNA molecule. They should become familiar with the Watson-Crick model of DNA structure, recognizing the significance of the nucleotide sequence in that it directs the activities of cells and determines the traits of the organism.

Students should examine the relationship between DNA, genes, chromosomes, and inheritable traits.

Grade 11
Micro-Unit 1153. At this level, students should understand the relationship of genes to DNA and proteins to traits in all organisms. They should examine how DNA sends its messages to the cell through RNA, and using Hammerling's experimental evidence, determine that the nucleus is the controlling factor. They should study the structure of RNA, noting how structure determines function.

Students should understand how genetic code and amino acid sequence determine a specific protein. They should examine the process of protein synthesis, using icons to represent cell organelles and the RNA molecules, and be able to apply this process to examples of recombinant DNA and genetic engineering.

Grade 12
Micro-Unit 1207. Antigens and antibody production in white blood cells can be studied at this level, including an introduction to introns and exons. Students should recognize the importance of protein synthesis to point mutations. They should explore how genetic engineering is applied to the production of antibodies and hormones. Using the operon model, they should examine the gene-regulatory functions of prokaryotic organisms.

Students should distinguish levels of organization in plants and animals. They should examine germination and fertilization and the development of an embryo in a higher plant or animal, particularly the development of the human embryo from fertilization of the egg to completion, focusing on germ layers and organ development.

Referring to aspects of comparative anatomy, students can identify types of reproduction and methods of development for different animals.

Matter, Energy, and Organization in Living Systems

(*NSES*, pp. 186–187)

Cell Energy Sources, ATP, and the Utilization of Energy

NSES Generalizations (p. 186)

The chemical bonds of food molecules contain energy. Energy is released when the bonds of food molecules are broken and new compounds with lower energy bonds are formed. Cells usually store this energy temporarily in phosphate bonds of a small high-energy compound called ATP.

The energy for life primarily derives from the sun. Plants capture energy by absorbing light and using it to form strong (covalent) chemical bonds between the atoms of carbon-containing (organic) molecules. These molecules can be used to assemble larger molecules with biological activity (including proteins, DNA, sugars, and fats). In addition, the energy stored in bonds between the atoms (chemical energy) can be used as sources of energy for life processes.

The distribution and abundance of organisms and populations in ecosystems are limited by the availability of matter and energy and the ability of the ecosystem to recycle materials.

Further Description:

Of prime importance to all cell activities is the ability of the cell to convert high energy yielding compounds, such as sugar, to a usable chemical energy. The chief source of energy in the cell is from carbohydrates. Carbohydrates are broken down in order to produce the energy molecule ATP. The process of conversion, referred to as cell respiration, takes place in the mitochondrion. In the presence of oxygen, glucose is oxidized by a series of enzyme-controlled reactions that provide the energy to synthesize many ATP molecules. ATP, in turn, will release the necessary energy for cell activities.

When oxygen is not present, this metabolic pathway is altered and glucose will yield a very small amount of energy with end products of alcohol or lactic acid. In yeast the process of producing alcohol is called fermentation.

Matter, Energy, and Organization in Living Systems
CELL ENERGY SOURCES, ATP, AND THE UTILIZATION OF ENERGY, CONT.

The health and maintenance of a population in any ecosystem is controlled by factors that limit its survival. Limiting factors influence a population in terms of density, range of distribution, dispersion patterns, and niche selection. An understanding of a population's range of tolerance to these factors becomes critical to an understanding of its status in an environment. Physical factors that tend to become limiting in either minimum or maximum quantities are light, temperature, water, required nutrients, atmospheric gases, space, currents, and pressure.

Concepts Needed:
Grade 9
Photosynthesis, cell respiration, carbohydrates, kilocalories, calories, temperature

Grade 10
Atmosphere, nutrients, bond energy, energy molecules, ATP, oxidation-reduction

Grade 11
Glycolysis, citric acid cycle, ATP, mitochondrion, membrane structure, oxidative phosphorylation, bond energy

Grade 12
Niche, habitat, limiting factors, range of tolerance, populations

Empirical Laws or Observed Relationships:
Law of the minimum, law of tolerance

Theories or Models:
Krebs cycle, chemiosmosis, glycolysis, oxidative phosphorylation, citric acid cycle

Learning Sequence, Grades 9–12:
Grade 9
See Micro-Unit 9.56, Biology, p. 120.

Grade 10
Micro-Unit 1049. Here students can examine the high-energy organic compounds—carbohydrates and lipids—and determine the calories of those groups. They should explore oxidation-reduction reactions, the energy of combustion, and energy in chemical bonds.

Matter, Energy, and Organization in Living Systems
CELL ENERGY SOURCES, ATP, AND THE UTILIZATION OF ENERGY, CONT.

Grade 11
Micro-Unit 1157. Students should examine the pathways of glycolysis, pyruvic acid, and the citric acid cycle, and study the bond energy of ATP. Oxidative phosphorylation and the proton-pump of mitochondrial membranes can be introduced.

Grade 12
Micro-Unit 1242(a). At this level, students should understand the significance of niche and habitat selection. They should analyze flow of energy and nutrient cycling as they occur in an ecosystem and how temperature and climate can determine the specific plant and animal populations that inhabit a particular ecosystem. They should recognize that temperature, quality of light, water, currents, and atmospheric pressure are major influences on development of biomass in the world.

Energy Flow Within and Between Living Systems
NSES Generalizations (pp. 186–187)

As matter and energy flow through different levels of organization of living system—cells, organs, organisms, communities—and between living systems and the physical environment, chemical elements are recombined in different ways. Each recombination results in storage and dissipation of energy into the environment as heat. Matter and energy are conserved in each change.

All matter tends toward more disorganized states. Living systems require a continuous input of energy to maintain their chemical and physical organizations. With death, and the cessation of energy input, living systems rapidly disintegrate.

The complexity and organization of organisms accommodates the need for obtaining, transforming, transporting, releasing, and eliminating the matter and energy used to sustain the organism.

Further Description:
All life, from the simplest cell to the most complex organism, requires a constant supply of energy to maintain itself. Most organisms receive their energy from sugar produced by photosynthesizing organisms.

Ecosystems as well require a continual input of energy from the sun in order to sustain community structure. The energy flow in all ecosystems sets

Matter, Energy, and Organization in Living Systems
ENERGY FLOW WITHIN AND BETWEEN LIVING SYSTEMS, CONT.

up a food pyramid from producers to consumers. A small amount of sunlight (1% to 3%) is converted by plants (producers). Only 10% of stored energy in plants is available to herbivores (primary consumers), and only 10% of that energy is available to secondary consumers. Much of the energy consumed is dissipated as heat through respiration of organisms. The productivity of any ecosystem is based on the amount of energy stored by the producers that can be passed on to consumers. Measurements of productivity must include rates of photosynthesis in excess of respiration.

All living systems require energy to be maintained. Death of protoplasm results in a "shutdown" of enzyme systems, DNA function, and all activities that require energy, such as growth, reproduction, and metabolism. A constant supply of energy is essential to maintain the activities of living systems. Energy production involves the transfer of electrons from atoms to molecules and from molecules to compounds. Living systems are more complex than what remains after death and the processes that follow death. The degenerated remains are far simpler and reflect an increase in entropy (greater disorder).

Metabolism is based upon the activities of living protoplasm. These activities and associated metabolism account for a continual rearrangement of electrons whereby energy is converted from one form to another. The laws of thermodynamics apply to every living system, from the simplest cell to the most complex organisms on Earth.

Concepts Needed:
Grade 9
Community, respiration, productivity, energy flow, food chain, biomass

Grade 10
Entropy, biomass, productivity, trophic levels, chemical cycles

Grade 11
Pyramids, models, productivity

Grade 12
Exergonic and endergonic reactions, entropy

Empirical Laws or Observed Relationships:
First and second laws of thermodynamics

Theories or Models:
Food chains, food webs, trophic pyramids, biomass, energy flow, ten percent law, Hutchinson productivity model

Matter, Energy, and Organization in Living Systems

ENERGY FLOW WITHIN AND BETWEEN LIVING SYSTEMS, CONT.

Learning Sequence, Grades 9–12:

Grade 9

Micro-Unit 952. Students should explore the concepts of food chain and food web and how these concepts relate to energy transference in an ecosystem.

Micro-Unit 953(a). Students should examine fundamental energy transfer along a typical food chain.

Grade 10

Micro-Unit 1048(b). Students should identify the carbon cycle as the main energy source for ecosystems. They should examine and compare the ecological pyramids of numbers, biomass, and energy and, using gross productivity models, be able to organize the specific trophic levels of ecosystems found in terrestrial and aquatic environments.

Grade 11

Micro-Unit 1145. Students should explore the laws of thermodynamics and their connections to living protoplasm. They should develop models of productivity.

Grade 12

Micro-Unit 1224. At this level, students should compare exergonic and endergonic reactions and interpret entropy as randomness. Looking at enzyme activities in human physiological functions, they should apply metabolism to changes in energy states.

The Molecular Basis of Heredity (*NSES*, p. 185)

Traits, Genes, Chromosomes, and DNA

NSES Generalizations (p. 185)

Most of the cells in a human contain two copies of each of 22 different chromosomes. In addition, there is a pair of chromosomes that determines sex: a female contains two X chromosomes and a male contains one X and one Y chromosome. Transmission of genetic information to offspring occurs through egg and sperm cells that contain only one representative from each chromosome pair. An egg and a sperm unite to form a new individual. The fact that the human body is formed from cells that contain two copies of each chromosome—and therefore two copies of each gene—explains many features of human heredity, such as how variations that are hidden in one generation can be expressed in the next.

In all organisms, the instructions for specifying the characteristics of the organism are carried in DNA, a large polymer formed from subunits of four kinds (A, G, C, and T). The chemical and structural properties of DNA explain how the genetic information that underlies heredity is both encoded in genes (as a string of molecular "letters") and replicated (by a templating mechanism). Each DNA molecule in a cell forms a single chromosome.

Changes in DNA (mutations) occur spontaneously at low rates. Some of these changes make no difference to the organism, whereas others can change cells and organisms. Only mutations in germ cells can create the variation that changes an organism's offspring.

SS&C Inferred Generalization (p. 185)

Recombinations and crossing over are also factors affecting mutation rates.

The Molecular Basis of Heredity
TRAITS, GENES, CHROMOSOMES, AND DNA, CONT.

Further Description:

Before DNA and chromosomes can be described, an understanding of variations, how these variations are induced, and the discreteness of these variations must be developed. This leads to correlating Mendel's observations with certain cellular events identified by Sutton.

Observing Traits. Examination of characteristics, the identification of a trait and how a trait varies, is of prime importance. Measuring the heights of humans provides a common experience for most individuals and lays the groundwork for distinguishing between continuous and discontinuous variations. These experiences lead to the concept of phenotype as an observable characteristic. No mention of DNA, genes, or chromosomes is necessary at this time. This type of study can be done in the middle level although it can be repeated in grade nine.

A question that evolves from this study of traits is one of whether traits are caused by heredity or caused by some environmental factor such as nutrition, exercise, or temperature. In addition, can there exist environmentally induced traits that can be passed on to subsequent generations? Studies of certain plant growth episodes and modern examples of this problem can be examined to provide evidence to reject these hypotheses. Lamarckism can be used as a hypothetical explanation for inheritance of traits. For example, the development of the giraffe's long neck as explained by Lamarck would involve each generation stretching and developing its neck and passing the development onto its offspring. This example should include the line of evidence that leads to its rejection as a viable explanation.

By examining traits, it is easy to observe some that are discrete and others that seem to demonstrate a blending. Analysis of human pedigrees will often reveal that some characteristics skip generations and do not produce individuals with an intermediate version of the trait. Other characteristics seem to exhibit a blending, somewhat as the blending of colored light or pigments. Certain plants offer easy systems to observe this blending and discreteness. It is also important to realize that traits are not always present in a single generation and may or may not be associated with gender. These observations provide evidence for sex-linked traits to be discussed later.

Mendelian Laws and Chromosomal Behavior. Students need to derive an understanding of chromosomal behavior from direct experiences. They can begin with F2 generations of green albino corn seedlings, soybean mutant strains, Tenebrio variants, fast plants, and, of course, the time-honored fruit flies. These studies would focus on Mendel's laws of segregation and

The Molecular Basis of Heredity
TRAITS, GENES, CHROMOSOMES, AND DNA, CONT.

independent assortment. Observing these "chance" events will provide students with a direct method of deriving these laws.

After deriving these basic rules, one must deal with the exceptions, that is, ratios that depart from 3:1 and 9:3:3:1, and demonstrate that these exceptions are just variations of the basic rules. Epistatic ratios and linkage are the two simple but interesting exceptions. It is not the deviation from the rules of independent assortment that is important. Rather, it is the interaction of gene pairs to produce epistatic ratios and the spatial relationship of genes to the linear configuration known as the chromosome.

By grade 10, evidence providing a correspondence between chromosomes and these Mendelian laws needs to be developed. This involves some model building. Meiosis and the behavior of chromosomes during anaphase I and anaphase II provide an explanation for independent assortment. Models using pipe cleaners and other materials could be used to represent the different chromosomes and traits. Examining the haploid systems of Neurospora or Sordaris increases the depth of understanding of these Mendelian laws.

Differences in chromosome number in humans and the resulting syndromes are interesting phenomena to students. However, unless students understand how chromosomes are gained or excluded in gamete production these syndromes lose much of their significance. Nondisjunction in fruit flies can be connected to sex-linked traits as the ultimate correlation of genes with chromosomes.

All organisms including humans have a specific number of chromosomes that helps define the species. Humans have 22 pairs of autosomes and two sex chromosomes. Chromosomes carry genes that will determine the characteristics of organisms. In humans the two sex chromosomes have an additional function—determining the sex of the individual. A female carries chromosomes designated as XX while a male carries chromosomes designated as XY. In the production of sex cells a female will produce an egg with 23 chromosomes. The 23rd chromosome will always be an X chromosome. Male sex cells or sperm will carry 23 chromosomes including either an X or a Y chromosome. If the X sperm cell fertilizes the egg the individual produced is a female (XX). If the Y sperm cell fertilizes the egg the individual produced is a male (XY). Therefore, in humans the male sex cells determine the sex of offspring.

Pedigree analysis of human sex-linked (X-linked) traits such as color vision, hemophilia, and glucose-6-phosphate dehydrogenase deficiency would provide evidence for the cellular basis of heredity. White-eyed fruit flies would also provide an example of this phenomenon. The mechanism of sex

The Molecular Basis of Heredity
TRAITS, GENES, CHROMOSOMES, AND DNA, CONT.

determination is also of great interest. What determines maleness—the absence of the Y chromosome or the presence of only one X chromosome? Do other animals have the same system?

Sex cell production in humans is a cellular process produced by specialized glands in the human body. In males the testes are responsible for producing sperm, and in females the ovaries are responsible for producing eggs. Sex cells are produced by meiosis, a process that reduces the number of chromosomes to exactly one-half the number of the original cell. Meiosis ensures that each sex cell will carry one but only one representative of each chromosome in the adult. Upon fertilization of egg and sperm, the offspring produced carries exactly half the traits of the male parent and half the traits of the female parent. During chromosomal movement, chromosomes segregate evenly into the sex cells through the process of meiosis.

Genes. At the lower level of abstraction, the gene has been described as simply a trait. This description is crude and inadequate when one has some understanding of the molecular basis of genetics. By grades 11 and 12, it is conceptually appropriate for the gene to be defined in terms of function. Evidence from nutritional mutant strains in yeast or molds and the study of biochemical pathways with accumulation products (PKU, alkaptonuria) provide evidence for this further definition. The empirical evidence of one gene equaling one enzyme (or better, protein) work of Beadle and Tatum can be done with appropriate microorganisms. The focus of these experiments is not to just repeat them but to build a model of how a gene functions.

Because chromosomes exist in pairs, genes will exist in pairs. Genes coding for the same trait can exist in different forms. Genes can be expressed in the outward appearance of an organism, or genes may be concealed. If a gene is expressed it is said to be dominant. If the gene is concealed it is said to be recessive. Many other interactions of genes may occur, for example, as incomplete dominance or blended characters and as codominance, where both characters are expressed. Many other types of gene expressions result in producing the tremendous variations found in one species.

DNA Structure. Building a model of the double helix does not provide much information for the model of the gene. From this discussion, genes have been correlated with chromosomes; the next question is one of structure and function. Of all the various chemical compounds within a cell, which is the genetic molecule and how can its structure support the

The Molecular Basis of Heredity

TRAITS, GENES, CHROMOSOMES, AND DNA, CONT.

requirements of genetic function? Experiments such as those of Avery; Hershey; and Chargaff are beneficial even to just read about. Finally, after all of this evidence has been gathered, the structure of DNA can be used to demonstrate that (1) it provides information for the production of the gene product; (2) it has coding ability; and (3) it has a self-replication mechanism.

DNA (and in some cases RNA) codes for all genetic traits in all organisms because it carries specific code sequences that are translated into traits through protein synthesis. The structure of the molecule allows for countless rearrangements of its units or codes. These codes arrange themselves into specific sequences that then determine traits. The arrangement of the sequences is infinite, and therefore the possibilities of different kinds of traits are unimaginable. An organism is made up of thousands of characteristics specific to its species. The genes that produce these traits are attached to chromosomes. Chromosomes are the structures that will carry traits from cell to cell and from parent to offspring. In order for genes to be copied, the DNA molecule must replicate itself. DNA replication is a process by which DNA can produce exact replicas of itself. Because of replication, identical genetic information is replicated and can be passed on from one generation to the next.

Mutations and Recombinant DNA. Recombinant DNA studies at this point would be appropriate and would provide students with experiences in manipulating the gene. Biotechnology and the importance of gene splicing can be easily discussed.

A sudden change in the genetic composition of an organism is called a mutation. Mutations are the agents for change in characteristics of any species and therefore are important for the origins of new species. Mutations are the direct result of structural changes of chromosomes or changes in the gene itself. Chromosomal changes include deletion, where a segment of a chromosome is missing, translocations, where a portion of a chromosome is broken off and attached to another chromosome, and inversions, where part of a chromosome is inverted with respect to the rest of the chromosome.

Structural changes in the gene result from substitution of one or more nucleotides of the genetic code. Regardless of the type of mutation that is produced, mutations provide variations from which natural selection can work. When mutations occur in the production of male and female sex cells, these mutations may be inherited through recombination of sex cells in fertilization.

The Molecular Basis of Heredity
TRAITS, GENES, CHROMOSOMES, AND DNA, CONT.

Concepts Needed:
Grade 9
Discontinuous variation, continuous variation, genetically determined variation, trait, phenotype, probability

Grade 10
Chromosomes, autosomes, sex chromosomes, sex cells, heredity, diploid, haploid, genotype, dominant and recessive, sex determination, sex-linked traits, mean, standard deviation

Grade 11
One gene equals one protein, DNA structure, DNA replication, DNA transcription, RNA function, protein synthesis, nucleus

Grade 12
Replication, amino acid sequence, code sequence, mutations, detection, inversion, translocation, point mutation, nucleotide, DNA structure, germ cells, recombination

Empirical Laws or Observed Relationships:
Principle of segregation, principle of independent assortment, meiosis, one gene–one enzyme, Chargaff rule, sexual reproduction, life cycle, polygenetic inheritance

Theories or Models:
Chromosome theory of inheritance, chromosome mapping, semiconservative hypothesis, base-pair complementarity, chi-square model, punnet squares

Learning Sequence, Grades 9–12:
Grade 9
Micro-Unit 902. Students should observe continuous variation and discontinuous variation and consider their causes. They can examine examples of discreteness and blending using certain plant and animal pedigrees.

Students should observe Mendelian principles of dominance, segregation, and independent assortment and experience these principles using Mendel's historical approach of "discrete factors." Punnet squares can be introduced to examine these crosses.

BIOLOGY 103

The Molecular Basis of Heredity

TRAITS, GENES, CHROMOSOMES, AND DNA, CONT.

Grade 10

Micro-Unit 1004. At this level, students can distinguish the autosomes from the sex chromosomes. They should examine the human genotype and chromosomal abnormalities associated with human genetic disease (autosomal), such as Down's syndrome.

Students should identify the sex cells, comparing and contrasting their production and characteristics in males and females. Due to unique genetic combinations, the male gamete determines the ultimate gender of the human embryo. Chromosomal abnormalities (linked to the sex chromosomes), such as Turner's and Klinefelter's syndromes, can be used to demonstrate problems with variations in the number of sex chromosomes.

Micro-Unit 1005. Students should distinguish between the phases of mitosis and meiosis, specifically in humans. They should examine the Mendelian principles of segregation and independent assortment and how they relate to meiosis, correlating chromosomal behavior with observations of segregation and independent assortment.

As they examine the structure of chromosomes and their action during meiosis, students should determine that sex cells contain half the amount of genetic information of one parent and half the amount of genetic information of the other parent. (Students should study basic probability and statistical significance, using the mean, standard deviation, and chi-square.)

Grade 11

Micro-Unit 1152. After the cellular basis of heredity has been demonstrated, the gene that until this time has been defined as a trait can be redefined in terms of its structure and function. The concept of one gene equaling one protein can be introduced along with the problem of mutations.

Next the question is posed of what chemical compound found in the cell could constitute this genetic molecule. By this time, students have clearly correlated genes with chromosomes and can determine that it must be one of the chemicals composing the chromosomes. Once they have identified these materials, they can examine them to see if the structure supports the genetic function required. Avery's identification in 1944 of component genetic material begins this study, followed first by Chargaff, and then by Meselson, Stahl, and Hershey.

The Molecular Basis of Heredity
TRAITS, GENES, CHROMOSOMES, AND DNA, CONT.

Different types of cells and their chromosomes can be examined to determine any differences. Prokaryotic and eukaryotic cells should be studied to see how their chromosomes differ. These differences lead to a study of the structure of eukaryotic chromosomes and ways in which chromosomes may be altered, deleted, and inverted. These alterations can be related to the importance of variability in a population. Mutations and their implications can be studied in conjunction with this topic.

Grade 12
Micro-Unit 1206. Building the double-helix structure of DNA using Watson and Crick's model appropriately occurs at this junction. More importantly, the structure of DNA can be studied to see how it and base pairing support the genetic coding mechanism. Exploring the process of DNA replication both with simplistic models and the semiconservative hypothesis provides further evidence of DNA's ability to fulfill the requirements of genetic information (self-replication). The need for this replication can be related to the process of simple cell division.

These activities lead naturally into a study of chromosome mapping and the abnormalities that can happen during the actions of chromosomes. Examination of how genes are mapped on chromosomes is appropriate as are investigations into recent advances in genetic research in the prevention of inherited diseases and gene therapy.

Genetic recombination studies and gene splicing can be examined along with modern molecular genetics. This is an opportunity for students to carry out studies involving genetic engineering and protein synthesis with a basis for understanding what they are doing.

Biological Evolution
(NSES, p. 185)

Natural Selection and Its Evolutionary Consequences
NSES **Generalizations** (p. 185)
Natural selection and its evolutionary consequences provide a scientific explanation for the fossil record of ancient life forms, as well as for the striking molecular similarities observed among the diverse species of living organisms.

The millions of different species of plants, animals, and microorganisms that live on Earth today are related by descent from common ancestors.

Further Description:
The fossil record is an accurate but very incomplete account of organisms that flourished on Earth millions of years ago. Through geological forces such as sedimentation and compression, the replaced remains of organisms, often as imprints, have produced fossil-bearing rock strata. This fossil rock record supplies scientific evidence that supports the Darwinian theory of natural selection by showing the continual replacement and displacement of species over geologic time. Darwin proposed the mechanism of "gradualism," whereby a species accumulates small changes over many generations. Improved forms would be selected while less improved forms would become extinct. Darwin hypothesized that the fossil record in rock would eventually uncover these "gradual" changes of species, showing an accurate account of their evolutionary history.

Recent evidence suggests, however, that gradualism is not totally supported by new fossil finds. It seems that fossil gaps are actually not flaws in the fossil record but a true picture of how species have originated. "Punctuated equilibrium" has been proposed as an explanation that supports the fossil rock record as an accurate account of evolutionary events. Fossil records indicate many species "maintain equilibrium" or remain unchanged and then "suddenly" new changes happen. These new forms come from preexisting ones and remain intact with little change for periods of long geological time until the next episode, or punctuation, takes place. To best understand these changes, they need to be tied to genetics and how such rapid changes might occur.

Biological Evolution
NATURAL SELECTION AND ITS EVOLUTIONARY CONSEQUENCES, CONT.

The fossil records not only indicate a catalog of species that have become extinct but also reveal the extent to which major groups are related to each other through homologies of common ancestry.

Descent from a common ancestry can be understood by examining avenues of speciation, namely phyletic change and cladogenesis. Phyletic change is based on the gradual accumulation of variations until a species no longer resembles its predecessors. Speciation has occurred because of selection acting upon new traits. These changes have been observed in fossil records, as exhibited in the phylogeny of the modern horse.

Cladogenesis connects ancestral origins through a splintering process. In this process the origin of a new species is the direct result of the isolation of small populations from ancestral stocks. Favorable genetic variations of ancestral populations were acted upon and increased quickly. Because the population was isolated, the variations would not be "diluted" and new species could develop.

Taken collectively and supported by the fossil remains, phyletic change and cladogenesis can result in adaptive radiation or evolution from a common ancestry to a number of different forms, each specialized to fill a different habitat and ecological niche.

Concepts Needed:
Grade 9
Fossils, geological forces, imprints, sedimentation, compression, rock strata, extinction, common descent, ancestral stock, natural selection

Grade 10
Homologous, analogous and vestigial structures, speciation, adaptive radiation, phylogeny

Grade 11
Carbon dating, radioactive decay, adaptive radiation

Grade 12
Speciation, founder effect, gene flow, geologic time table

Empirical Laws or Observed Relationships:
Rates of change in certain key elements (e.g., carbon-14, and the ratio of lead-206 to uranium-238 in rocks or the ratio of trapped helium to radium) give us methods to date fossils and minerals. (The results of such measurements show Earth to be approximately 4.5 billion years old.) DNA and

Biological Evolution
NATURAL SELECTION AND ITS EVOLUTIONARY CONSEQUENCES, CONT.

immunological relatedness; the assembly of facts of evolutionary change; nested hierarchies or similarity for morphological and DNA characters, which show that evolution has resulted in a branching tree of diversification.

Theories or Models:
Natural selection, gradualism, punctuated equilibrium, law of superposition, law of cross-cutting relationships, law of evaluded fragments, descent with modification, cladogenesis, phyletic change, divergent and convergent evolution

Learning Sequence, Grades 9–12:
Grade 9
Micro-Unit 905. Students should explore homologies of animals that reveal common ancestry. They should also consider how structures without a common evolutionary origin can be similar in function but not in structure (give examples, such as the wings of birds and insects).

Micro-Unit 907. Students should study the rock cycle and how fossil rocks form. They should examine common fossils of plants and animals and the process of fossil formation dealing with replacement of remains, fossil traces, and original remains.

Grade 10
Micro-Unit 1003. Students should review examples of homologous, analogous, and vestigial structures. They should distinguish between divergent and convergent evolution as they relate to natural selection. They should also examine phyletic trees of major groups of plants and animals and the isolating mechanisms that cause speciation.

Grade 11
Micro-Unit 1105. Students should examine the radioactive decay of elements, including the concepts of half-life as a measurement of the age of rock and radiocarbon dating as a measurement of the age of fossils. They should study the geological time scale connecting higher taxonomic groups, examining natural selection and the extinction of organisms.

Students should define gradualism as the classical interpretation of fossil records and consider "punctuated equilibrium" as a possible alternative to gradualism.

Biological Evolution

NATURAL SELECTION AND ITS EVOLUTIONARY CONSEQUENCES, CONT.

Grade 12

Micro-Unit 1215. Students should explore the major evolutionary changes occurring in eras of the geological time table. They should examine the mechanisms involved in modes of speciation and the importance of the founder effect upon the origin of new forms.

Students should identify the major patterns of adaptive radiation seen in the fossil records and in modern groups living today. They should note distinctive trends in primate evolution, with an emphasis on the hominids and human evolution.

Biological Classifications: Their Basis in Evolutionary Relationships

NSES Generalizations (p. 185)

Biological classifications are based on how organisms are related. Organisms are classified into a hierarchy of groups and subgroups based on similarities which reflect their evolutionary relationships. Species is the most fundamental unit of classification.

The great diversity of organisms is the result of more than 3.5 billion years of evolution that has filled every available niche with life forms.

Further Description:

Observations of the structural diversity of organisms lead to an understanding of the commonality of structure and function. The great diversity of organisms on Earth is classified into a hierarchy of groups and subgroups based on similarities of external and internal structure, chemical makeup, and evolutionary relationships. The most basic unit is the species, which in sexually reproducing populations consists of organisms that successfully reproduce among themselves. The classification system most commonly used today separates organisms into five major groups called kingdoms. The five kingdoms are: Monera, Protista, Fungi, Plantae, and Animalia. Kingdoms are further divided into subgroups.

The scheme used to classify organisms was devised by the eighteenth century Swedish naturalist Carolus Linnaeus. Linnaeus developed what he called the binomial system for naming organisms. According to his scheme, the scientific naming of organisms consists of two parts—the genus, which contains one species or a group of similar species, and the specific epithet (usually an adjective), which in some way describes the genus. Both names taken together denote the species name.

Biological Evolution

BIOLOGICAL CLASSIFICATIONS, CONT.

Biologically speaking, a species can be considered as (1) a reproductive unit whereby individuals of the same species are reproductively isolated from all other groups; (2) an ecological unit in that a species will interact with other species; and (3) a genetic unit consisting of inheritable traits and variations of those traits being selected from generation to generation.

The grouping of organisms into a hierarchical scheme is known as taxonomy. Each category in a taxonomic scheme defines an important set of characteristics unified according to phylogeny or common ancestry. Common descent should indicate similar genes, and hence, similar characteristics. This may not always be the case. Selective pressures of the environment may cause different species that are unrelated to have similar characteristics. Likewise, phylogenetically related organisms may have dissimilar characteristics.

Biological diversity can be understood in terms of the number of different kinds of organisms living in today's world. This diversity of species can be grouped into five major categories—from bacteria and protists, Earth's earliest life forms, to the diversification of multicellular plants, animals, and fungi. The large number of different kinds of organisms is the direct result of selective pressures on a great variety of body forms, behavioral responses, and physiological activities. Through selection, variations of individuals within a species have the opportunity to occupy, successfully or unsuccessfully, a wide range of habitats found on this planet. Successful variations compete better and will be maintained through reproductive success. Many millions of years of selection, driven by environmental pressures placed upon variations within a population, have resulted in the adaptation of millions of new forms. Because the environment is constantly in flux, variations are continually being tested and new species added to this tremendous catalog of life on Earth.

Much about the structure and function of life forms comes from comparative anatomy, comparative embryology, and comparative biochemistry.

Concepts Needed:

Grade 9
Binomial nomenclature, genus, species, hierarchical scheme, classification, taxonomy, reproduction, kingdoms, inheritance, characteristics

Grade 10
Prokaryotic cells, eukaryotic cells, life cycles, haploid, diploid, meiosis, growth

Grade 11
Sporophyte, gametophyte, embryonic development, common descent, organization of body forms, alteration of generations, symmetry

Biological Evolution

BIOLOGICAL CLASSIFICATIONS, CONT.

Grade 12
Molecular taxonomy, cladogram, geologic time scale, plant and animal diversity

Empirical Laws or Observed Relationships:
Observations of similar characteristics for organisms—homologies (characters similar due to shared descent) vs. analogies (characters similar because of parallel adaptation or chance); geostratification; increased diversity and complexity of living organisms over time; the rate of evolutionary change differs dramatically among different groups of organisms, and from one geologic era to another, as well as among genes of different function.

Theories or Models:
Systematics, monophylogeny, polyphylogeny, numerical phenetics, cladistics, amino acid sequencing, DNA sequencing, punctuated equilibrium

Learning Sequence, Grades 9–12:
Grade 9
Micro-Unit 901. Students should understand that a characteristic is a feature that a thing has that can be used in identifying it whereas a trait is a more specific and more narrowly defined characteristic. They should understand how organisms can be categorized based on similar characteristics and that a series of these categories, each of which is called a taxon, makes up a classification system.

Students should learn the scheme of hierarchy at the kingdom level—plants, animals, bacteria, fungi, and protists. They can also examine the behavioral patterns of various organisms

Grade 10
Micro-Unit 1001. Students should examine the organization of body forms, from single-celled protists to colonial forms to complex multicellular organisms. They should organize the major divisions of plants and animals, showing phylogenetic similarities, and explore life-cycle concepts, including distinctions between the haploid and diploid conditions of plants and animals.

Micro-Unit 1055. Students should identify prokaryotes as organisms with cells that lack membrane-bound internal structures, understanding that most are one-celled organisms. They should identify eukaryotes as organisms that have cells containing internal, membrane-bound structures. (They can be either one-celled or many celled.)

Biological Evolution

BIOLOGICAL CLASSIFICATIONS, CONT.

Grade 11

Micro-Unit 1101. Students should compare plant and animal phylogeny. They should explore alternation of generations in plants, distinguishing primitive, transitory, and complex life cycles, and the evolutionary trends of gametophytes and sporophytes. In animals, students should examine the distinctive phylogeny of major groups, emphasizing symmetry and embryonic germ development.

Grade 12

Micro-Unit 1208. Students should compare the classical view of taxonomy with modern systematics, distinguishing their different methodologies. They should construct a cladogram of common groups of plants and animals and compare their nucleotide and amino acid sequences.

At this level, students should be able to produce an approximate evolutionary time scale indicating the appearance of life on Earth and the roles of bacteria, algae, and plants.

Processes of Evolution: Mutation, Recombination, and Natural Selection

NSES Generalization (p. 185)

Species evolve over time. Evolution is the consequence of the interactions of (1) the potential for a species to increase its numbers, (2) the genetic variability of offspring due to mutation and recombination of genes, (3) a finite supply of the resources required for life, and (4) the ensuing selection by the environment of those offspring better able to survive and leave offspring.

Further Description:

Darwinian fitness is based upon the natural selection of random chance variations in a gene pool of a population. The selection process allows for "favorable" genetic variations to better compete. Individuals carrying these variations are better able to take advantage of unexplored habitats or may require different biological or physical aspects of their niche. These variations are then inherited through sexual reproduction.

Variations that enable individuals to produce more offspring are considered to be "most fit." These variations become more frequent with each generation. Over time, individuals carrying fit variations can speciate. Speciation occurs when individuals become genetically isolated from other groups by conditions that prevent interbreeding.

Biological Evolution

MUTATION, RECOMBINATION, AND NATURAL SELECTION, CONT.

Concepts Needed:

Grade 9
Reproduction, variability, adaptation, niche, habitat

Grade 10
Recombination, speciation, mutation, adaptation, selective pressures, adaptive radiation, convergent evolution, divergent evolution, parallel evolution

Grade 11
Variability, common descent, fitness, inheritance, Lamarckism

Grade 12
Gene pool, genetic drift, pre- and post-mating isolating mechanisms, geographic isolation, allele frequency, gene mutations, chromosomal mutations, speciation, gradualism, punctuation

Empirical Laws or Observed Relationships:

Many traits show high heritability, that is, similarity between parents and offspring; this evidence suggests that some variation for that trait is genetically based. Environmental influences on individuals can also produce important variation, but that variation is not observed to be inherited and cannot drive evolution or adaptation. Phenotypic variation equals genetic variation plus environmental variation.

Theories or Models:

Natural selection, modes of speciation, allopatry and sympatry, disruptive selection, stabilizing selection, directional selection, Hardy-Weinberg law, genetic drift, founder effect, heterozygote superiority

Learning Sequence, Grades 9–12:

Grade 9

Micro-Unit 903. Students should observe variations found among individuals of the same species, understanding how certain variations enhance the survival of organisms in their environment.

Micro-Unit 904. Students should explore the adaptive connections of organisms with their niches and habitats.

Biological Evolution
MUTATION, RECOMBINATION, AND NATURAL SELECTION, CONT.

Grade 10
Micro-Unit 1002. Students should observe the phenotypic expressions of mutations and determine their evolutionary significance in terms of "fitness." They should examine the processes of genetic variability, including mutations, crossing over, and sexual recombination. They can study the genetic basis of evolution by examining artificial breeding experiments.

Grade 11
Micro-Unit 1103. Students should examine and compare Darwin's theories of variability, common descent, inheritance, and fitness. The question of whether these traits are environmentally induced or inherited provides a study of Lamarckism and is very effective at this time.

Grade 12
Micro-Unit 1216. Students should distinguish between the gene flow of a population and genetic drift. They should explore steady state of gene inheritance with Hardy-Weinberg equilibrium and the mechanisms of selection stabilizing, disruptive and directional selection on variability in a species, and convergent evolution.

Students should compare distinctive modes of reproductive isolation, as in pre-and post-mating mechanisms, and examine allopatric and sympatric speciation and adaptive radiation.

The Interdependence of Organisms (NSES, p. 186)

Cycles in the Biosphere and Energy Flow Through Ecosystems

NSES Generalizations (p. 186)

The atoms and molecules on the earth cycle among the living and nonliving components of the biosphere.

Energy flows through ecosystems in one direction, from photosynthetic organisms to herbivores to carnivores and decomposers.

Further Description:

The cycling of nutrients in any ecosystem is essential to maintain a balance in that ecosystem. Ecosystems are dependent upon resources that are used by organisms and the recycling of wastes disposed by them. Essentially the same atoms and molecules are being used over and over again. Nutrient cycling of organic and inorganic substances takes place in all ecosystems. Nutrients critical for maintaining homeostasis in any ecosystem are carbon, nitrogen, and phosphorus.

The carbon cycle begins with atmospheric CO2, which is absorbed by plants. CO2 is fixed through photosynthesis into glucose, which is used by all organisms in respiration to produce ATP. In respiration, CO2 is released as a waste product and sent back to the atmosphere. This cycle sets up the basic food chain for all ecosystems. CO_2 is released into the atmosphere through decomposition and combustion as well, adding to the reservoir of CO2 necessary to continue this cycle.

The nitrogen cycle is based upon the action of the decomposers in soil. Decomposers have the ability to convert nitrogen wastes and dead organic matter into a usable form for plants. In addition, a special group of nitrogen-fixing bacteria can convert nitrogen gas from the atmosphere into nitrates.

The phosphorous cycle is a sedimentary cycle; that is, rock containing small amounts of phosphorous is eroded and phosphorous then becomes available to plants. Animals take in phosphorous from the food web, use it in making ATP and DNA, and through excretion, release it as a waste. Bound-up phosphorous is released into the soil by decomposers.

The Interdependence of Organisms
CYCLES IN THE BIOSPHERE, CONT.

Water, essential for all life, must also be cycled. The cycling of water occurs through evaporation, condensation, and precipitation. The sun causes evaporation from the oceans and lakes as well as transpiration from plants. Water is carried to the atmosphere condensed and falls in the form of rain or snow. The amount of precipitation helps define the type of ecosystem that will exist in a particular geographic region.

The fuel for ecosystems is the sun's energy. This radiant energy is captured by plants and converted into a usable form of chemical energy, namely glucose. Energy flow in ecosystems occurs when the primary producers (plants) carrying this energy are eaten by herbivores (animals that eat only plants), which in turn are eaten by carnivores (animals that eat only animals). This sets up what is known as a food chain. Food chains, however, are usually rare. In most ecosystems food chains usually become food webs. A web occurs when one or more levels of the food chain interconnect with other levels for their food supply. Food webs are usually complex and can define niche adaptations in ecosystems.

Concepts Needed:
Grade 9
Biotic, abiotic, biosphere, natural resources, organic compound and inorganic compound, decomposition, condensation, precipitation, microorganisms, photosynthesis, carbon cycles, energy flow, producers, consumers, herbivores, carnivores, omnivores, food chains, food webs, habitat, niche, decomposers

Grade 10
Predator-prey dynamics, carbon cycle, ecosystem, trophic structure

Grade 11
Phosphorous cycle, carbon cycle, nitrogen cycle, human waste disposal and fossil fuel consumption

Grade 12
Decomposers, trophic levels, heat budgets, energetics

Empirical Laws or Observed Relationships:
Conservation of matter, first and second laws of thermodynamics

Theories or Models:
Trophic pyramids, food web, hydrologic cycle, carbon cycle, nitrogen cycle, phosphorous cycle

The Interdependence of Organisms
CYCLES IN THE BIOSPHERE, CONT.

Learning Sequence, Grades 9–12:

Grade 9
Micro-Unit 953(b). Students should examine food chain relationships and the importance of inorganic compounds. They can study the water cycle, including transpiration by plants, as an important factor in the maintenance of ecosystems.

Micro-Unit 954. Students should explore the relationships of plants, animals, fungi, bacteria, and protists to the trophic pyramids, placing these groups into trophic levels as producers, consumers, secondary consumers, tertiary consumers, and decomposers.

Grade 10
Micro-Unit 1030. Students should examine flow of energy and nutrient cycling as they occur in an ecosystem and how temperature and climate can determine the specific plant and animal populations that inhabit a particular ecosystem. They should understand that temperature, quality of light, water, currents and atmospheric pressure are major influences on development of biomass in the world.

Micro-Unit 1048(a). Students should identify the basic components of the carbon cycle as the critical pathway for energy transference, based on the photosynthesis model. They should understand the actions of bonding atoms (ionic and covalent bonds).

Micro-Unit 1048(c). Students should compare inorganic compounds with organic compounds necessary for nutrient cycling in ecosystems.

Grade 11
Micro-Unit 1142. Students should identify the soil nutrients essential for ecosystem maintenance and distinguish among the critical biochemical cycles—nitrogen, phosphorous, and carbon (including chemical reactions of these cycles and microorganisms that control these pathways). They should understand the human impact of waste runoff and fossil fuel combustion as it relates to these cycles.

Grade 12
Micro-Unit 1243. Students should compare energy relationships found in aquatic and terrestrial ecosystems and relate these to habitat and niche adaptations. They can study the efficiency of energy flow in various ecosystems and predatory-prey relationships in energy flow models.

The Interdependence of Organisms
CYCLES IN THE BIOSPHERE, CONT.

Students should investigate the role of decomposers in the maintenance of energy flow. They can also explore how energetics and adaptations relate to balancing heat budgets or conserving energy.

Organisms, Ecosystems, and Population Growth: Interrelationships and Interdependencies

NSES Generalizations (p. 186)

Organisms both cooperate and compete in ecosystems. The interrelationships and interdependencies of these organisms may generate ecosystems that are stable for hundreds or thousands of years.

Living organisms have the capacity to produce populations of infinite size, but environments and resources are finite. This fundamental tension has profound effects on the interactions between organisms.

Human beings live within the world's ecosystems. Increasingly, humans modify ecosystems as a result of population growth, technology, and consumption. Human destruction of habitats through direct harvesting, pollution, atmospheric changes, and other factors is threatening current global stability, and if not addressed, ecosystems will be irreversibly damaged.

Further Description:

The organization of ecosystems is based upon populations interacting with each other and with abiotic factors of the environment. The interaction of populations sets up a community. Populations may interact in positive or negative ways. An example of a positive interaction is seen in the pollinating activities of flowering plants. In this symbiosis, the flower is fertilized while the pollinator collects its food.

Predator-prey relationships show a positive as well as negative association. Competition for resources can also cause negative interaction. In this case the population most affected by the competition is eliminated from a niche. Because of these interactions, numerous adaptations have evolved that prevent elimination of populations from a selected ecosystem. Species have adapted to be able to coexist with each other by sharing resources, reducing competition, and entering into positive symbioses.

In any community, populations will tend to replace each other in an orderly process. This is due to the fact that habitat populations change. Use of nutrients and other "abiotic" factors by resident populations causes habitats to change, resulting in a replacement process, or succession. This process of

The Interdependence of Organisms

ORGANISMS, ECOSYSTEMS, AND POPULATION GROWTH, CONT.

community change results in a series of transitory communities until a final or mature community is established. Given sufficient time and stability of biotic and abiotic factors, a climax will be reached. The climax community can last for hundreds of years uninterrupted.

All populations have an inherent tendency to increase in size. This potential increase is extremely high for most species. This type of exponential growth begins slowly and then continues on a rapid incline as more reproductive individuals are produced each generation. Control of population growth is based upon limiting factors and population interactions in each ecosystem. Resources such as food, water, oxygen, and space availability, as well as predation, competition, and parasitism, place environmental limits on population growth. These limits set the carrying capacity of the ecosystem. Population size will oscillate around this carrying capacity. When a population exceeds carrying capacity, a strain upon resources could result in a sharp decline in the population.

Human civilization has brought about dramatic changes in the ecosystems of the world. These changes have resulted in major environmental problems, which in turn directly affect the survival of all species on Earth. Because of agricultural practices, technological advances, and medical triumphs, world population growth has reached a size well over 5 billion. This "population explosion," coupled with a lack of understanding of ecological principles, has resulted in massive pollution of land and water, destruction of habitats and loss of bio-diversity, possible climate changes that could result in global warming, and penetration of the protective ozone layer shielding all life from harmful UV rays. Policy decisions facing planet Earth should focus on population control, recycling of human waste, and development of alternative energy sources, and should develop a better understanding of the human impact on ecosystem balance.

Concepts Needed:
Grade 9
Population, community, niche, habitat, competition, ecosystem, limiting factors, exponential growth mortality

Grade 10
Succession, serial stages, ecotone, pioneer species, climax communities, associations, community

Grade 11
Symbiosis, predator-prey, mutualism, amensalism, commensalism, parasitism, succession, biotic potential, agriculture, technology, human population

The Interdependence of Organisms

ORGANISMS, ECOSYSTEMS, AND POPULATION GROWTH, CONT.

growth form, biodiversity, layers of the atmosphere, waste disposal, fossil fuels, recycling, pesticides, pollutants, endangered species, abiotic factors

Grade 12
Density-dependent and density-independent factors, carrying capacity, acid rain, ozone depletion, succession, climax concept

Empirical Laws or Observed Relationships:
Interdependence, population levels of species fluctuate with environmental conditions

Theories or Models:
Competitive exclusion principle, equilibrium hypothesis of island biogeography, climax communities, facilitation hypothesis, inhibition hypothesis, J-shaped and S-shaped growth form, age distribution pyramids, r and K strategies, global warming, succession

Learning Sequence, Grades 9–12:

Grade 9
Micro-Unit 955. Students should explore the concept of population as it relates to ecosystems.

Micro-Unit 956. Students should examine limiting factors and the various areas where limiting factors are applicable, including how they affect population growth. (Focus on light, water, and mineral nutrients.)

Grade 10
None suggested.

Grade 11
Micro-Unit 1143. Students should examine aspects of succession, looking at primary and secondary succession models and distinguishing serial stages of representative terrestrial ecosystems.

Grade 12
Micro-Unit 1242(b). Students should distinguish between the "law" of the minimum and the "law" of tolerance, examining the range of tolerance that a species may exhibit and how specific limiting factors will determine its distribution. They should understand density-dependent and density independent factors affecting populations.

The Interdependence of Organisms
ORGANISMS, ECOSYSTEMS, AND POPULATION GROWTH, CONT.

Micro-Unit 1244. Students should compare density-dependent and density-independent factors and distinguish between a climate climax theory and a polyclimax theory. Looking at representatives of the plant and animal kingdom, they should examine the population characteristics of natality, mortality, abiotic potential, and age distribution. They can relate the concept of carrying capacity to that of limiting factors.

Students should understand the equation for exponential growth, $dN/dt = rN/(K-N)/K$ and identify concrete examples found in nature that show this experimental exponential growth. They should apply the equation to human population growth in various countries of the world (analyzing age-pyramids of human populations in these various countries).

Students can also explore the effects of human population growth on natural resources, including issues such as biological magnification, ozone depletion, eutrophication, acid rain, deforestation, global warming, and toxic and radioactive waste.

The Behavior of Organisms

(*NSES*, p. 187)

Stimuli, Receptors, Nervous Systems, Responses, and Behavior

NSES Generalizations (p. 187)

Organisms have behavioral responses to internal changes and to external stimuli. Responses to external stimuli can result from interactions with the organism's own species and others, as well as environmental changes; these responses can be either innate or learned. The broad patterns of behavior exhibited by animals have evolved to ensure reproductive success. Animals often live in unpredictable environments, and so their behavior must be flexible enough to deal with uncertainty and change. Plants also respond to stimuli.

Multicellular animals have nervous systems to generate behavior. Nervous systems are formed from specialized cells that conduct signals rapidly through the long cell extensions that make up nerves. The nerve cells communicate with each other by secreting specific excitatory and inhibitory molecules. In sense organs, specialized cells detect light, sound, and specific chemicals and enable animals to monitor what is going on in the world around them.

Like other aspects of an organism's biology, behaviors have evolved through natural selection. Behaviors often have an adaptive logic when viewed in terms of evolutionary principles.

Behavioral biology has implications for humans, as it provides links to psychology, sociology, and anthropology.

Further Description:

In animals the evolution of a nervous system that allowed for communication of the internal environment of an organism with external stimuli became highly adaptive. The development of a nervous system allowed animals the opportunity to move more easily, which in turn gave them advantages in activities such as food gathering and escaping from predators. These actions

The Behavior of Organisms
STIMULI, RECEPTORS, NERVOUS SYSTEMS, RESPONSES, AND BEHAVIOR, CONT.

evolved into behavioral responses. As animals became more complex, so did their nervous systems and their responses to environmental stimuli. Organisms respond to internal changes and to external stimuli. Responses to external stimuli can result from interactions with the organism's own species and others, as well as from environmental changes. The broad patterns of responses exhibited by organisms have evolved to ensure reproductive success. Organisms often live in unpredictable environments, and so their responses must be flexible enough to deal with uncertainty and change.

Like other aspects of an organism's biology, behavioral patterns have evolved through natural selection. The adaptive nature of many behavioral patterns is apparent when viewed in the context of evolutionary principles.

The nervous system is based on the structure of the neuron, or the nerve cell. Basically, neurons can be classified into two groups—sensory neurons, which respond to light, heat, pressure, or chemicals in the environment; and motor neurons, which carry information to areas of the animal's body for appropriate response. Chemical compounds called neurotransmitters can excite or inhibit responses of nerve cells. By releasing neurotransmitters, nerve cells regulate the physiological functions of the organism.

A complex sensory system evolved in animals. This system allowed for the interpretation of many selective environmental stimuli. Without this system animals could not maintain homeostasis with their environments. The sensory system allowed for the innovation of what is commonly known as the five senses—touch, taste, smell, sound, and sight. Sensory systems have become highly adapted. In complex animals behavioral responses such as courtship, mating habits, nesting, food gathering, and communication have become integrated with sensory systems.

Behavioral patterns in animals are based on genes that have been selected because of their positive response to environmental stimuli. Behavior is a naturally selective process. In selection the "fit" characteristics in some way contribute to the survival of individuals and allow them to increase in number. Behavioral responses directly or indirectly parallel reproductive success.

A response can be instinctive, that is, genetically programmed, or it can be learned, which means that it has been acquired or eliminated as a result of experience. With instinctive behavior patterns, nervous reflex becomes an automatic response to a stimulus. A sense receptor in some way has been activated, and a reflexive act or what is known as a fixed action pattern occurs. It is understood, however, that this reflex is adaptive and has been naturally selected.

The Behavior of Organisms
STIMULI, RECEPTORS, NERVOUS SYSTEMS, RESPONSES, AND BEHAVIOR, CONT.

In learned behavioral responses, animals adjust their behavior patterns through experience. Examples of learning behavior are habituation, where organisms cease to respond to stimuli that are not important to them; conditional learning, where the organism learns by continuous exposure to one stimulus; and imprinting, where a learned response takes place at a brief critical period in the early life of an animal when there is exposure to a specific trait of one or both of the parents. Learned behavior is adaptive as well because it gives animals an opportunity to adjust to new environmental changes. Behavior has a genetic basis.

Concepts Needed:
Grade 9
Nervous systems, neuron, motor nerves, sensory nerves, behavior, learning, stimulus, homeostasis

Grade 10
Neurotransmitters, voltage, depolarization, repolarization, stimulation, impulse, membrane potential, action potential, threshold, all-or-none response, imprinting, conditional reflex

Grade 11
Active transport, sodium pump, refractory period

Grade 12
Neurotransmitters, neuromuscular synapse, summation, CNS, PNS, sensory system, fixed action pattern, tropisms

Empirical Laws or Observed Relationships:
Electrochemical transmission of synaptic signals, the Weber-Fechner law (the stimulus needed to be perceived is proportional to the stimulus acting), genetic and molecular bases of behavior

Theories or Models:
Sodium-potassium pump and membrane potential, proximate and ultimate causation, special behavior, kin selection, selfish gene, altruism

Learning Sequence, Grades 9–12:
Grade 9
Micro-Unit 911. Students should observe the specialized structures of neurons and the nervous system of a simple animal.

The Behavior of Organisms

STIMULI, RECEPTORS, NERVOUS SYSTEMS, RESPONSES, AND BEHAVIOR, CONT.

Micro-Unit 912 Students should examine types of behavioral responses found in the animal world and common behavioral responses that occur in humans. They can measure the strength of various stimuli needed to perceive changes (pressure, light intensity, sound intensity, concentration of lemon juice in water solution).

Grade 10
None suggested.

Grade 11
Micro-Unit 1160. Here students should distinguish between the sensory and motor aspects of a reflex arc and identify the primary functions of the central and autonomic nervous systems. They should examine the major sensory organs of the human body, including the eye and the ear

Animal responses to environmental stimuli can be introduced by looking at classic studies of learned behavior, such as imprinting and conditioned responses. Students can explore stages of socialization in animals, comparing invertebrate to vertebrate societies and kin selection in higher animals. The hypothesis of a selfish gene also can be introduced.

Grade 12
Micro-Unit 1217. Examination of the specialized cells of the human nervous system is appropriate here. Students should study the structure of the neuron and nerve impulse transmission in relation to the sodium-potassium pump process. They should examine neurotransmitters and their effects on nerve impulses and the action of the sodium-potassium pump at neuromuscular junctions in human muscle cells.

Micro-Unit 1218. At this level, students can infer the logarithmic character of the Weber-Fechner law and relate that to the use of decibels in sound, magnitudes of stars, and pH as a logarithmic quantity.

Earth/Space

NSES Topics

Energy in the Earth System

Geochemical Cycles

The Origin and Evolution of the Earth System

The Origin and Evolution of the Universe

Energy in the Earth System (NSES, p. 189)

Heat from Within Earth and Heat from the Sun

NSES Generalization (p. 189)

Earth systems have both internal and external sources of energy, both of which create heat. The sun is the major external source of energy.

Further Description:

Since the sun is a variable star, its solar output varies slightly over short time periods. Solar disturbances such as flares, prominences, and sunspots increase the amount of radiation from the sun. However, no long-term variations in the intensity of solar radiation have been measured at altitudes above Earth's atmosphere. Solar radiation, at about 1,400 W/m^2, varies by no more than 2%. In contrast, the geothermal heat flow from Earth averages only about 0.061 W/m^2. Some theories have related climatic changes to sunspot cycles (11 years) and magnetic cycles (22 years), but no clear connection has yet been established between climate and sunspots or magnetic cycles.

The sun emits energy as electromagnetic radiation. Unlike sound, such radiation requires no medium, therefore this energy is able to travel through the near vacuum of space from the sun to the earth.

Most radiant energy from the sun is concentrated in the visible and near-visible parts of the EM spectrum, and it peaks at about 500 nm, very near the 555 nm visibility peak for *Homo sapiens,* a result which surely is not a coincidence (and is connected to evolution). Less than 1% of solar radiation is emitted as X-rays, gamma rays, and radio waves.

Only about 25%, or about 350 W/m^2, of incoming solar radiation penetrates the transparent atmosphere of the earth. The remainder is either absorbed by the atmosphere or scattered back into space. There are some latitudinal differences found on Earth. These variations are determined by time of year, by the wavelength of the energy being transmitted, and by the depth and nature of the intervening material.

Terrestrial radiation is produced mainly as a result of reradiation of solar radiation. The energy is absorbed from the sun as the sun's spectrum but reradiated from Earth at the much longer wavelengths associated with the

Energy in the Earth System

HEAT FROM WITHIN EARTH AND HEAT FROM THE SUN, CONT.

temperature of Earth. The Wien displacement law, in which the wavelength is inversely proportional to the absolute temperature, provides a comparison of those peak wavelengths.

Since the sun has a surface temperature 20 times greater than that of Earth, the reradiated energy has a spectrum that peaks at a wavelength 20 times longer than the 500 nm for the sun, or at about 10,000 nm, well into the infrared. Since the atmosphere is more absorptive to such long-wavelength terrestrial radiation, the atmosphere is heated from the ground up instead of vice versa.

In addition, water vapor and carbon dioxide absorb the long wavelengths of radiation from the earth especially well, leading to the so-called "greenhouse" effect. (The temperature in real greenhouses rises mainly because the glass prevents the heated air from rising, thereby increasing the temperature inside.) Ozone, on the other hand, absorbs only very short wavelengths, mainly in the ultraviolet range, and therefore forms a shield of sorts, absorbing much of the ultraviolet radiation before it can reach the earth.

Radiation from the sun follows an inverse square law, so that comparisons of the solar constant can be made for other planets if we know their mean distances from the sun in AU. For example, Mars is 1.93 times further from the sun than is Earth. Its solar constant should therefore be about 27% that of Earth, about 374 W/m^2. Because there is little atmosphere to absorb the energy, this is about the same as what we receive at the surface of Earth.

Spacecraft have provided us with temperature measurements for both Mars and Venus. Mars has an average temperature of about 5 °C, whereas Venus has a temperature of about 500 °C. Earth is about 1.4 times further away from the sun than is Venus, and we would expect from the inverse square law that it would receive about twice as much radiation. The fact that its temperature is so much greater can be attributed only to greenhouse warming.

Winter and summer seasons on Earth are a consequence not just of the obliquity factor associated with the sun's rays, but also of the longer days during the summer than during the winter. Of course, both of these factors are a consequence of the 23.5 degree tilt of Earth's axis of rotation with the plane of its orbit about the sun.

The sun's radiation travels at the speed of light, and all wavelengths travel at that speed in a vacuum. When there is dispersion, some wavelengths travel at slightly different speeds than others. That is how we are able to form a spectrum with a glass prism, since blue light slows down in glass slightly more than does red light.

Energy in the Earth System

HEAT FROM WITHIN EARTH AND HEAT FROM THE SUN, CONT.

The methods of heat transfer—conduction, radiation, and convection (advection)—allow heat to be transferred and to ultimately warm the earth's atmosphere. Convection is particularly important to air heating and consequent movements in the atmosphere.

A balance is maintained between incoming solar radiation and the amount of terrestrial radiation. This is usually referred to as the heat budget. If this balance is disrupted, Earth will become progressively colder or warmer.

The inverse square law can be used to find the total energy per second emitted by the sun, and we can compare that number to how much energy per kilogram we would get from chemical burning. We can show that whatever is happening on the sun, it is not chemical burning. Other considerations are the constancy of the sun's spectral lines and its mass over the span of human existence. Thus, we must explore the source of the sun's energy, which is nuclear in its origins. This leads to a consideration of nuclear fusion, which requires an understanding of nuclear theory and special relativity (Einstein's energy equation).

Concepts Needed:
Grade 9
Energy, radiation, wavelength, spectrum, convection, conduction, temperature, calorie, seasons, orbit, Earth tilt, scattering, reflection, absorption, prism, dispersion

Grade 10
Latitude, longitude, orbit, altitude, azimuth

Grade 11
Seasons, earth tilt, heat budget

Grade 12
Corona, chromosphere, photosphere, convection zone

Empirical Laws or Observed Relationships:
Inverse square law, Wien displacement law, mechanical equivalent of heat

Theories or Models:
Electromagnetic theory, Stefan-Boltzmann radiation law, atomic and molecular theories, nuclear theories

Energy in the Earth System

HEAT FROM WITHIN EARTH AND HEAT FROM THE SUN, CONT.

Learning Sequence, Grades 9–12:

Grade 9

Micro-Unit 926. Students should secure air temperature measurements in a variety of atmospheric conditions, as this data can provide some evidence of the effects of heat.

Micro-Unit 938. Students must be able to measure temperature and understand units of heat, initially in calories, since that unit is easily connected to the heating of water. For students to understand these concepts and relationships they must experiment with both heat and heat transfer and the sun as a source of energy that produces heat.

Micro-Unit 939(b). Students should study heat and heat transfer through a variety of heat transfer experiments. These heat experiments need to provide evidence to support the existence of the transfer methods—convection, conduction, and radiation. Providing simulations is helpful but (more importantly) what evidence do we have that heat travels in these ways? Various materials can be exposed to sunlight to observe heat absorption. Such materials can also be considered from the point of view of heat being reradiated.

Micro-Unit 947. Students should understand that the sun is the primary external source of energy for Earth. They should examine the effects of the basic processes by which a substance (including Earth) absorbs radiation at one set of wavelengths and reradiates that energy at longer wavelengths, understanding that this process is largely responsible for the heating of the atmosphere and Earth's surface and surroundings.

Micro-Unit 949(d). Students should observe the sun and produce its spectrum with a grating or prism. They should understand the qualitative connection between the sun's spectral distribution and one produced by a thin wire that is heated by current from a battery, from the point that it just feels hot (deep, invisible infrared) until it is red in appearance (indicating a peak in the infrared).

Grade 10

Micro-Unit 1008. Students at this level should measure the position and altitude of the sun at noon and examine the variation of sunset position over time. They should examine the relative position and appearance of the sun over the year at different geographical locations and understand the consequences of the sun's orientation with respect to the earth's temperature.

Energy in the Earth System

EARTH'S INTERNAL ENERGY SOURCES

Grade 11

Micro-Unit 1123. Students in grade 11 should understand the earth-moon system, including the position of the moon in relationship to the earth.

Micro-Unit 1125. After their experiences in the ninth and tenth grades, students can now provide evidence for the cause of the seasons. This evidence should include the position of the sun at noon over time and the variations in sunset positions.

Micro-Unit 1139. By this time, students need to develop an understanding of the earth's heat budget, varying heat capacities of earth materials, and latitudinal heat balances. Basic landsat maps can provide views of these heat differences. They should understand the mechanical equivalent of heat so that heat energy can be expressed in joules, and the concept of power in watts.

Grade 12

Micro-Unit 1230. Students should use Wien's displacement law to consider peak wavelengths of radiators of various temperatures. They should compare predicted and actual temperatures on various planets based upon their relative distances from the sun, and examine discrepancies in these predictions in terms of greenhouse gases and atmospheric pressures on those planets.

Micro-Unit 1231. At this point students should understand how the sun produces energy and how its structure supports these processes. They should examine quantitatively the fourth power radiation law and fission and fusion in terms of Einstein's energy equation. They should also study the chemistry, spectral energy characteristics, and kinetics associated with ozone, water vapor, and carbon dioxide in the atmosphere.

Earth's Internal Energy Sources: Radioactivity and Gravitational Energy

NSES Generalization (p. 189)

Two primary sources of internal energy are the decay of radioactive isotopes and the gravitational energy from the earth's original formation.

Further Description:

When Becquerel (1896) accidentally placed a uranium sample on a photographic plate, he found the plate to be partially exposed. This startling discovery led to the discovery of radioactivity. Materials that are radioactive contain

Energy in the Earth System
EARTH'S INTERNAL ENERGY SOURCES, CONT.

atoms whose nuclei split apart, giving off energy and charged particles. As the nuclei break apart, the resulting radiation is absorbed by matter to produce heat. In many cases the radiation is in the form of extremely short-wavelength gamma radiation, and also there are often particles, alpha (helium nuclei) or beta (electrons), that can have considerable energies. These radiations and particles interact with other particles, transferring energy that ultimately becomes heat in the material that has absorbed the radiation. This is the form of heat that warms the interior of the earth. This radioactive decay produces energy, and a more stable element is formed.

Although Earth's average heat from radioactivity and the original gravitational sources is extremely small on the average compared with energy from the sun, there are "hot spots" around Earth. (Gravitational heat is energy released when masses aggregate, converting their original potential energy due to their separation into heat energy.) The original gravitational heat, along with the production of heat by radioactivity in the earth, is still very substantial, so much so that at depths of 30–50 km, the temperature is more than 500 °C. It is especially interesting that heat flow decreases with the age of ocean floors or continental areas. This decrease is connected to fundamental properties of radioactivity—half-life and mean lifetime, which allow us to date these areas.

Certain minerals contain radioactive elements, and the rates at which these elements decay can be determined and used to date events in Earth's history. Radioactive decay is a measure of geological absolute time. Boltwood, an American chemist, first devised a method of using radioactivity to determine the age of a substance. He found that you could calculate the age if you compared the amount of the parent material (such as uranium) contained in a sample with the amount of the decay product (in the case of uranium the stable product is lead-206). For ancient rocks, only four radioactive isotopes are helpful. They are uranium-238, uranium-235, potassium-40, and rubidium-87. Most of these elements occur in igneous rocks. Uranium-238 is the most commonly used radioactive isotope in this dating process. Its half-life is 4.5 billion years.

Carbon-14, with a half-life of 5,730 years, allows us to date rocks formed more recently and to date organic material. This radioactive isotope is produced in the upper atmosphere and mixes with regular carbon dioxide in the atmosphere. The ratio of carbon-14 to regular carbon is very constant. Living organisms continuously exchange carbon atoms with their surroundings, so that the ratio is constant in living matter as long as it is alive. As soon as the living matter dies, it no longer replaces the carbon and the ratio begins to decrease as radioactive decay of carbon-14 occurs. The amount of activity then indicates the date when the living matter died. Similarly, carbon-14

Energy in the Earth System
EARTH'S INTERNAL ENERGY SOURCES, CONT.

atoms in certain rocks will decay. Thus, the ratio of radioactive to regular carbon dioxide molecules gives a measure of age of the sample.

The decay products of uranium-238 include eight alpha particles, beta decay, and gamma decay. An alpha particle is composed of two protons and two neutrons. A beta particle is an electron that is emitted from the neutrons in the nucleus. Uranium-238 decays through a chain of other transformations, ultimately producing lead-206 and eight helium atoms. Since helium gas is produced, one method of dating samples is to measure the amount of helium gas trapped in a rock with U-238 and lead. Since the half-life of uranium is 4.5 billion years, a gram of U-238 would produce so few decays per year that the heat produced would be only about 3.2 joules of energy per year per gram of U-238. This seems as though it is a very small amount of heat; however, even at 60 mW per square meter, heat coming from the earth's interior amounts to about 9×1020 J/year. If all of this heat were produced by U-238 decay, it would require that only 0.00046% of the earth's mass be U-238, perhaps not an unreasonable number. A study of radioactive decay provides some clues to the structure of the earth's interior. In addition, it provides clues to the earth's formation.

Residual gravitational energy is very difficult to study. It is largely associated with the molten inner core of the earth, which cannot be a source of additional heat. Earth matter that is carried to the surface brings much of this heat, and in that sense the original source—gravitational potential energy—is being observed.

Concepts Needed:

Grade 9
Radioactivity (as a macroscopic phenomenon), half-life, mean lifetime, density, mantle, crust, core

Grade 10
Radioactivity, radioactive isotopes, half-life, radioactive decay, nuclear reactions

Grade 11
Isotopes, radioactive, core (inner and outer), mantle, crust, internal structure, chemical composition of Earth

Grade 12
Parent/daughter isotope, alpha particle, beta decay, gamma decay, gravity, magma

Energy in the Earth System

EARTH'S INTERNAL ENERGY SOURCES, CONT.

Empirical Laws or Observed Relationships:
Law of universal gravitation, inverse square law for radiation, exponential absorption law for radiation, Earth's internal heat flux as a function of the age of ocean floors or continental regions

Theories or Models:
Mantle convection, evolution of Earth (physical), structure of Earth's interior

Learning Sequence, Grades 9–12:

Grade 9
Micro-Unit 939(a). Grade nine students can study the heat produced in or coming from inside Earth. This includes the high temperatures of deep mines, volcanoes, geothermal vents, etc. (like videos taken from underwater robots).

Micro-Unit 966(b). Using radioactive count data in a graph, students should determine half-life and mean lifetime of a radioactive sample.

Grade 10
Micro-Unit 1058. Using half-life data for various radioactive isotopes such as uranium-238 and carbon-14, students should compute simple ratios to determine ages of rocks or organic materials. The fact that one atom can change into another leading to sustained chemical chain reactions should be considered regarding its impact on science. This can be done by examining Marie Curie's research on the discovery of radium.

Grade 11
Micro-Unit 1108. Students should understand how age correlates with heat flux from radioactivity in Earth. When such data are correlated with other relative dating techniques, students will gain confidence in age estimates for Earth.

Grade 12
Micro-Unit 1245. Detailed processes associated with radioactivity can be examined at this point, including the nature of particles and energies emitted, how particles are detected and energies measured, and how such radioactivity interacts with matter. Students should understand radioactive dating techniques, including assumptions made for the various techniques.

Students should also determine the heat produced by various radioactive processes, estimating how much activity is required for a given amount of

EARTH/SPACE 135

Energy in the Earth System
EARTH'S INTERNAL ENERGY SOURCES, CONT.

heat produced. For example, knowing that the average heat flux from Earth is 60 milliwatts per square meter, knowing the area of Earth, and knowing how much energy is produced by the decay of a U-238 nucleus, an estimate can be made of how much activity is present, assuming that all of the heat flux is associated with radioactivity.

Convection in Earth's Mantle, Oceans, and Atmosphere

NSES Generalizations (p. 189)
The outward transfer of earth's internal heat drives convection circulation in the mantle that propels the plates comprising earth's surface across the face of the globe.

Heating of earth's surface and atmosphere by the sun drives convection within the atmosphere and oceans, producing winds and ocean currents.

Further Description:
There are two vastly different kinds of heat transformation systems. In the Earth, the amount of heat on the average is very small relative to that from the sun. The processes inside Earth are also mostly very slow, some requiring thousands to millions of years. Others, like volcanoes and earthquakes, require months to hundreds of years for any given location. The sun's energy absorbed and reradiated by Earth, which provides heat to interact with the oceans and atmosphere, involves transformations that occur much more rapidly than those inside Earth. Also, the total amount of energy from the sun is far greater.

Energy from the sun powers many of the gigantic cycles found on Earth. One of these is the hydrologic cycle, which provides a continuous exchange of water between the oceans, the atmosphere, and the continents. The energy from the sun also creates pressure and temperature differences on Earth's surface that, in turn, produce winds. Large-scale global wind patterns are a result of this interaction. These winds provide the energy for the production of surface waves and ocean currents. Small-scale wind patterns such as land and sea breezes are also connected with differential heating and resulting variations in pressure.

Storms such as hurricanes draw on this energy stored in the oceans. A hurricane's wind patterns and development progress through a series of

Energy in the Earth System

CONVECTION IN EARTH'S MANTLE, OCEANS, AND ATMOSPHERE, CONT.

stages. Winds become more organized in their cyclonic pattern and grow stronger. The hurricane moves across the earth's surface in response to pressure differences, as latent heat released during condensation drives the storm. The warm ocean provides the water vapor. Once on land a hurricane quickly dissipates because its source of energy is no longer available.

The physical movements of the ocean, such as currents and waves, can be studied to show the connection between the wind and these movements. Buffering of various substances also is affected by changes in the hydrosphere. Evaporation and indirect effects of wind change certain concentrations. Marine life also is affected by these winds, movements, and chemical buffering. Due to their mode of living, organisms are found in certain oceanic habitats.

Seismic waves are the major mechanism by which Earth's interior can be examined. Such waves can be interpreted in terms of refraction, reflection, wave speed, dispersion, and diffraction. From these wave properties, inferences of seismic disturbances provide a wealth of data about Earth's interior.

Seismic studies of the interior of the earth support the existence of "plastic" areas that allow convection movements. These plastic areas, although still solid, would be hot enough to flow in the typical circular pattern. Harry Hess (1960s) proposed that these convection cells acted as conveyor belts. Material rising at the ridges moves toward the trenches, carrying the sea floor with it. This model is supported by the relative youthfulness of the oceanic crust at the ridges as compared to its age in the trenches. Paleomagnetism studies further support this hypothesis.

The theory of plate tectonics provides a way to explain the earth's internal behavior, including patterns of earthquakes, faults and volcanoes on the earth's surface. Oceanic features such as the ridges, trenches, sea mounts, and rift valleys also are seen to have important functions on the surface. Igneous rocks of various types (FeMg silicates) can be identified and provide clues to the movement and existence of plates.

Concepts Needed:

Grade 9
Convection, speed and wave speed, wavelength, period, frequency, s (transverse) and P (longitudinal) waves, refraction, reflection, sea waves

Grade 10
Convection, subduction, plate boundaries, continent, ocean basin, rift zone,

Energy in the Earth System
CONVECTION IN EARTH'S MANTLE, OCEANS, AND ATMOSPHERE, CONT.

midocean ridge, volcanoes, earthquakes, faults, brittle, plastic, transform, trailing edge, collision edge, continental drift, plate tectonics, barometer, barometric pressure, isobars, temperature, precipitation, climate zones, global wind patterns, humidity, condensation, evaporation, transpiration, air masses, fronts, storms, inclination, rotation

Grade 11
Lithosphere, asthenosphere, Moho discontinuity, basalt, granite, andesite, viscosity, isostacy, paleomagnetism, sediments, subduction, ocean bottom structure

Grade 12
High pressure, low pressure, cyclones, hurricanes, currents, fronts

Empirical Laws or Observed Relationships:
Convection of solids, plasticity of solids, partial melting, conservation of energy, formation of currents, seismic transmission, reflection and refraction, continental drift

Theories or Models:
Theory of hurricane development, plate tectonics, gravity, origin and early history of Earth, models of Earth's interior structure and composition

Learning Sequence, Grades 9–12:
Grade 9
Micro-Unit 910(b). Much of the evidence supporting plate tectonics is connected to other areas of science. Some density studies could be conducted in grade nine to support later development of the model of Earth's interior.

Micro-Unit 940. Experiments dealing with the heat capacity of water would be helpful to demonstrate the heat reservoir nature of the ocean.

Micro-Unit 948. Students should understand concepts of convection of large masses of material within Earth, and they should understand the same concepts in regard to air and water masses on Earth's surface. They must possess a working knowledge of radiation, conduction, evaporation, latent heat, density, climate, weather, water masses, basic kinematics, currents, salinity, heat capacity of water (heat reservoir-ocean), ecosystems, and habitats. A study of oceanic habitats and ecosystems could be done at this time. More than likely, some of this work has been done at the middle level.

Energy in the Earth System

CONVECTION IN EARTH'S MANTLE, OCEANS, AND ATMOSPHERE, CONT.

Wave tanks can easily be used to simulate wave development and other coastal features.

Grade 10

Micro-Unit 1020. Grade 10 students should understand continental drift first as hypothesis, later as empirical law, and examine other evidence that can be fit into the framework of the theory of plate tectonics. They should recognize that major earth processes such as earthquakes, volcanic eruptions, and other natural disasters are associated with plate boundaries.

Students should understand that convective processes affecting the crust produces convergent and divergent plate boundaries, and they should be able to locate these major plate boundaries.

Micro-Unit 1023. Students should understand barometric pressure, as well as how to measure pressure with a barometer, how to chart isobars, and what isobars mean in terms of air movement on Earth. Weather maps can be used for this purpose.

Micro-Unit 1031(b). Students should identify factors that affect temperature locally, including proximity to water, elevation, insolation, insulation, surface types, unequal heating of Earth's surface, and hours of sunlight. Satellite imagery can provide information for these localized effects.

Grade 11

Micro-Unit 1115. Students should understand the effects of adiabatic lapse rate and its impact upon the atmosphere.

Micro-Unit 1150. A careful study of the sea floor spreading process, including an examination of the evidence provided by paleomagnetism and sediment ages, is appropriate at this time.

Grade 12

Micro-Unit 1204. After a study of pressure, storms, and air masses, students should identify fronts and predict movements. They should understand adiabatic lapse rates and other characteristic meteorological variables.

Micro-Unit 1239. The effects of specialized currents such as El Niño can be studied at this point.

Energy in the Earth System

GLOBAL CLIMATE: THE SUN'S ENERGY / DYNAMIC AND STATIC FACTORS

Global Climate: The Sun's Energy and the Influence of Dynamic and Static Factors

NSES Generalization (p. 189)

Global climate is determined by energy transfer from the sun at and near the earth's surface. This energy transfer is influenced by dynamic processes such as cloud cover and the earth's rotation, and static conditions such as the position of mountain ranges and oceans.

Further Description:

Global climate refers to the average weather of the entire earth over long periods of time (between 20 or 30 years). Climate is affected by the same processes as those in weather, but the time over which data are gathered is much greater. As a result, climate patterns have been identified, and there are attempts to correlate them with some process or change. The depletion of the ozone layer and the suggested climatic effects is one example of such a correlation. The heat transfer processes associated with seasonal fluctuations in the amount of solar energy reaching a given place on Earth's surface at a given time of year are caused by variations in the angle (inclination) of the sun's rays and by length of daylight (rotation). Both of these effects are due to Earth's inclination with respect to its orbital plane.

On a small scale, atmospheric conditions such as cloud cover, dust loading, and physiographic features also contribute to heat differences. Clouds are very good absorbers of terrestrial radiation and are primarily responsible for maintaining Earth's surface temperatures during the night. A thick cloud cover will absorb most terrestrial radiation, and a portion of this radiation is returned to Earth's surface. It is not surprising that on clear, dry nights the surface cools considerably more than on cloudy humid evenings.

Local conditions are affected, in some part, by the static features nearby. These features, such as mountains, oceans, and lakes, can modify the heat transfer process and the weather for that area. The specific heat of water, for example, provides large bodies of water with the ability to moderate climates of nearby land masses, since the water can exchange large amounts of heat with the air masses that pass over that land. Thus bodies of water form a buffer.

Concepts Needed:

Grade 9
Pressure, buoyancy, density

Grade 10
Albedo, insolation, insulation, atmospheric gases

Energy in the Earth System

GLOBAL CLIMATE: THE SUN'S ENERGY / DYNAMIC AND STATIC FACTORS, CONT.

Grade 11
Ozone, saturation, convective stability, vertical mixing, inversion, adiabatic, isothermal, isobaric, gradient

Grade 12
Climatology, warming planet, modeling, ice ages

Empirical Laws or Observed Relationships:
Stratification and lapse rates; adiabatic processes in the atmosphere; stability and instability of air masses; Coriolis effects on wind; geostrophic wind is inversely proportional to the distance between isobars; geostrophic winds flow as fluids, with no divergence or convergence.

Theories or Models:
Climatic cycles, climate models using computers

Learning Sequence, Grades 9–12:

Grade 9
Micro-Unit 927. Grade nine students should understand basic kinematics, velocity, and acceleration and their relationships in the context of atmospheric air masses (that contain water vapor). In this same context, they should examine pressure, temperature, the ideal gas law qualitatively, and the relationship between density of an air mass and its buoyancy. The basic concepts of heat and temperature and phase changes for water are essential.

Grade 10
Micro-Unit 1031(a). At this grade level students should recognize the factors that influence Earth's energy balance. Factors to consider on a planet scale include: distance from the sun, albedo, insulation, atmospheric composition of gases, and characteristics of the planetary surface. Satellite imagery can provide information for these planetary effects.

Grade 11
Micro-Unit 1116. Students should consider ozone in the thermosphere in terms of its ability to provide partial shielding from ultraviolet radiation from the sun. They should also have some familiarity with the process by which ozone is depleted by some CFCs.

Energy in the Earth System
GLOBAL CLIMATE: THE SUN'S ENERGY / DYNAMIC AND STATIC FACTORS, CONT.

Grade 12

Micro-Unit 1241. Grade 12 students should develop a broad view of climatology and how it affects Earth. A study of data and processes used by climatologists provides a strong foundation for the study of past and future climate changes. Data indicating ice ages and warming trends should be used.

Geochemical Cycles

(*NSES*, p. 189)

The Movement of Elements and Compounds Among Earth's Chemical Reservoirs

NSES Generalizations (p. 189)

The earth is a system containing essentially a fixed amount of each stable chemical atom or element. Each element can exist in several different chemical reservoirs. Each element on earth moves among reservoirs in the solid earth, oceans, atmosphere, and organisms as part of geochemical cycles.

Movement of matter between reservoirs is driven by the earth's internal and external sources of energy. These movements are often accompanied by a change in the physical and chemical properties of matter. Carbon, for example, occurs in carbonate rocks such as limestone, in the atmosphere as carbon dioxide gas, in water as dissolved carbon dioxide, and in all organisms as complex molecules that control the chemistry of life.

Further Description

Earth is a system containing essentially fixed amounts of each stable chemical element, except radioactive elements and the stable end products of radioactive decay processes. Water as a compound exists almost in a fixed amount on Earth. Each of these substances can exist in and move cyclically among several different chemical "reservoirs" in the solid earth, hydrosphere, atmosphere, and biosphere.

Movement of matter between "reservoirs" is driven by Earth's internal and external sources of energy. These movements are often accompanied by physical and chemical changes. Carbon, for example, occurs in rocks as limestone, in the atmosphere as a gas, in water as dissolved carbon dioxide, in coal and petroleum as hydrocarbons, in mines as diamond, and in all living things as organic molecules. Water occurs in various physical states and chemical mixtures as it cycles on and through the solid earth, atmosphere,

Geochemical Cycles
MOVEMENT OF ELEMENTS AND COMPOUNDS AMONG EARTH'S RESERVOIRS, CONT.

hydrosphere, and biosphere. Rocks, too, progress through a cycle in which different minerals are produced in different chemical and physical milieus.

Chemical cycles are common in nature and tend to recycle resources through the atmosphere, hydrosphere, solid earth, and biosphere. Elements from a nonliving environment (abiotic), such as rocks, air, and water, are cycled into the bodies of living organisms and then back into the nonliving environment. For example, nitrogen that once may have been part of a dinosaur may eventually form part of human DNA and still later become part of a tomato. The main geochemical cycles are carbon, phosphorous, nitrogen, water, and oxygen.

The carbon cycle involves the processes of photosynthesis and respiration. Carbon dioxide plays an important role in photosynthesis. Plants use energy from light to split water molecules; they then use carbon dioxide to synthesize carbohydrates. One of the products of this reaction is oxygen. Photosynthesis is the major source of oxygen in Earth's atmosphere. For some 1.5 billion years before green plants were on Earth, algae and bacteria provided the photosynthesis needed to build Earth's oxygen levels to the point that respiration of both plants and animals could occur.

Respiration, which occurs in both plants and animals, breaks up food molecules to obtain energy. It is the opposite process to photosynthesis, and at the cellular level it is connected to photosynthesis as a consequence of evolution. Photosynthesis and respiration form a major mechanism for the cycling of carbon. Part of the carbon cycle also involves the storage of carbon in the form of fuels and the storage of excess carbon dioxide in saltwater as carbonate. Carbon found in fuels is released through combustion. Carbonate is a main ingredient in the shells of ocean creatures and a large group of sedimentary rocks.

Nitrogen is an element that is often a limiting factor for plant growth. Although atmospheric nitrogen is abundant, it is not in a form that plants can readily access. The nitrogen molecule found in the atmosphere must be split and recombined with atoms to form molecules that are soluble in water. This is called nitrogen fixation. Typically nitrogen is fixed in the form of ammonium or nitrate ions. Some of this fixing occurs in the atmosphere due to lightning. Most nitrogen is fixed by bacteria. When plants and other organisms die, through leaching and the activities of other bacteria the nitrogen is returned to the atmosphere ready to begin the cycle again.

The water cycle is powered by the sun and cycles water through the oceans, glaciers, groundwater, freshwater rivers, and lakes. Through the processes of evaporation, transpiration, condensation, precipitation, infiltration, and runoff, water is cycled through our system and very little new water is added.

Geochemical Cycles

MOVEMENT OF ELEMENTS AND COMPOUNDS AMONG EARTH'S RESERVOIRS, CONT.

Oxygen also is involved in a cycle in which water is split through the process of photosynthesis to produce oxygen and carbon dioxide is used to synthesize carbohydrates. This oxygen is then used by animals and plants through respiration and by oxidation processes like burning to produce carbon dioxide—which, in turn, is needed for photosynthesis. Oxygen is capable of combining with almost all other elements and forms many oxides. These oxides can be found in rocks and minerals.

Phosphorous is involved in a lesser known chemical cycle. As these elements and compounds move through their cycles, physical and chemical changes occur. Water easily changes state, and many of the elements form related ions and complex compounds. Rocks are involved in many of these cycles. In a rock cycle, rock is transformed from one rock type into another. All of these cycles ultimately are powered by the sun.

Concepts Needed:

Grade 9
Chemical cycles, hydrologic cycle, transpiration, perspiration

Grade 10
Carbon cycle, precipitation, limestone, fossil fuels, coal, petroleum, porosity, permeability, traps, water budget, energy requirements

Grade 11
Condensation, evaporation, freezing, precipitation, latent heat of condensation

Grade 12
Cyclones, energy transfer

Empirical Laws or Observed Relationships:
Chemical reactions: oxidation-reduction, carbon cycle, rock cycle, nitrogen cycle, hydrologic cycle

Theories or Models:
First and second laws of thermodynamics, models of cycles

Learning Sequence, Grades 9–12:

Grade 9
Micro-Unit 941. Based on their knowledge of chemistry and biology, students should understand various cycles and their associated energy transformations. They should examine how weather is affected, as well as perspira-

Geochemical Cycles
MOVEMENT OF ELEMENTS AND COMPOUNDS AMONG EARTH'S RESERVOIRS, CONT.

tion cooling of animals, the transpiration effects on plants, and the conditions that drive storms.

Grade 10

Micro-Unit 1027. A study of energy production and energy requirements will help students recognize the importance of fossil fuels. They should examine types of fossil fuels, how they are formed, and how they are located and used. Environmental concerns such as acid rain and contamination of water reservoirs associated with fossil fuels can be addressed.

Micro-Unit 1032. The impact of water use and abuse can be addressed at this point with an analysis of water budget data.

Micro-Unit 1045(a). Students should examine the components of the carbon cycle, understanding that carbon dioxide dissolves in water and later precipitates out in the form of limestone. They should understand the relationships of cycles, as in the case of the association of carbon dioxide with calcium carbonate in the carbon cycle and with calcium carbonate in the rock cycle.

Grade 11

Micro-Unit 1114. Focusing on the conditions that drive storms, students should follow the movement of water through the water cycle.

Grade 12

Micro-Unit 1240. Students should explore the formation of cyclones and severe storms and the energy that drives them.

The Origin and Evolution of the Earth System (NSES, pp. 189–190)

The Origin and Age of the Earth: Rock Sequences, Fossils, and Radioactive Decay

NSES Generalizations (p. 189)

The sun, the earth, and the rest of the solar system formed from a nebular cloud of dust and gas 4.6 billion years ago. The early earth was very different from the planet we live on today.

Geologic time can be estimated by observing rock sequences and using fossils to correlate the sequences at various locations. Current methods include using the known decay rates of radioactive isotopes present in rocks to measure the time since the rock was formed.

Further Description:

An accepted model or theory for how the sun was formed is as follows. The sun was formed from a large interstellar cloud. As the cloud became denser, its own inward gravitational forces were stronger than the outward forces of the pressure. The cloud began to shrink, and the early sun or protosun began to form (a little more than 4.6 billion years ago). As this cloud contracted, the material within it was rotating in one direction and collecting most of its mass toward the center. As material collapsed into the center of rotation, conservation of angular momentum caused the cloud to rotate faster and faster, while the outer parts of the cloud flattened into a disk.

The Helmholtz theory suggests that the cloud's central temperature was approximately 10 million Kelvin, which initiated nuclear reactions. With the onset of these reactions a star was born, and it became more than just a ball of gas. In the outer parts of the cloud, a disk of gas formed that was as big as the solar system. The disk-shaped nebula (a cloud of gas and dust) that surrounded the contracting sun was called the solar nebula. This explanation is consistent with the basic laws of physics and has been somewhat confirmed through stellar observations and measurements, which show stars at various stages of this sequence.

Origin and Evolution of the Earth System

ORIGIN AND AGE OF THE EARTH, CONT.

Planets in the solar system differ in their compositions. The metal-rich planets lie closest to the sun (terrestrial planets), and the hydrogen-rich planets are farthest from the sun (Jovian planets). A condensation sequence can explain the appearance of certain minerals in certain planets. This difference in composition can be attributed to the distance of the planet from the sun and to the description of the solar system's formation. The composition of meteorites provides evidence for this early history of the solar system and supports the theory of mineral condensation.

As these solid grains and ices (composing the contracting interstellar clouds) condensed, planetesimals formed. Some collided with others and aggregated into larger bodies. The largest bodies survived, and moons formed in a similar process near these planetesimals. In the inner part of the solar system, collisions occurred until planets from the size of Mercury to Earth were formed. Most of these inner planets are composed of silicate material. The outer planets, or Jovians (giants), formed from ice as well as rocky material. Their masses grew much larger than those of the terrestrial planets, resulting in the development of a massive gaseous atmosphere.

The distances between most of the planets (we exclude Pluto, which is believed to have been captured, and include the asteroid belt) are found to be predictable through an empirical law, Bode's rule. This predictability was used as evidence to support the existence of some of the outer planets. Until telescope technology improved, planets such as Pluto could not be seen, but their existence was predicted by Bode's rule. Asteroids, comets, and meteorites provide further clues to the history of the early solar system. The scale of the solar system and the sizes of the planets are important because their dimensions and scalar relationships support the proposed descriptions of the solar system's formational history.

Concepts Needed:

Grade 9
Geologic time, relative time, fossils, periods, eras

Grade 10
Scale of solar system, Galileo, geocentric theory, heliocentric theory, meteorites

Grade 11
Absolute time, relative time, correlation, half-life

Origin and Evolution of the Earth System

ORIGIN AND AGE OF THE EARTH, CONT.

Grade 12
Protosun, protoplanet, absolute and relative time, nebulae, solar system, critical mass, coalescence, condensation sequence, scale of the solar system, comets, asteroids

Empirical Laws or Observed Relationships:
Bode's rule

Theories or Models:
Nebular hypothesis, law of universal gravitation, Helmholtz theory

Learning Sequence, Grades 9–12:

Grade 9
Micro-Unit 966(d). Grade nine students should learn to use the concept of geologic time in relationship to fossils.

Grade 10
Micro-Unit 1013. Students should construct and use scale models of the solar system to explain motions of planets and their moons and their apparent size and movement around Earth. Direct observations can be made using telescopes and binoculars.

Students should trace the historical difficulty in gaining acceptance for the evidence against the geocentric theory (Galileo).

Micro-Unit 1046(a). A comparison of the characteristics of Venus, Earth, and Mars will provide students with a view of the evolutionary nature of planets. Students should understand evidence for the existence, location, and chemical compositions of planets in our solar system. This evidence should include recent information from NASA or other modern sources as well as historical material. It should also include some spectral data and evidence from meteorites.

Grade 11
Micro-Unit 1106. Students at this level should relate relative time to absolute time, using both correlation of stratigraphic units and half-life data.

Grade 12
Micro-Unit 1233. Students should now be able to use chemistry and physics principles to consider aspects of stellar evolution: the condensation sequence, Helmholtz contraction, and the detailed history of the solar system.

EARTH/SPACE

Origin and Evolution of the Earth System
INTERACTIONS AMONG ECOSYSTEMS

Interactions Among Ecosystems: Earthquakes, Volcanoes, Mountain and Plate Movements

NSES Generalization (pp. 189–190)
Interactions among the solid earth, the oceans, the atmosphere, and organisms have resulted in the ongoing evolution of the earth system. We can observe some changes such as earthquakes and volcanic eruptions on a human time scale, but many processes such as mountain building and plate movements take place over hundreds of millions of years.

Further Description:
Just as life on Earth has been evolving, so has the solid earth, hydrosphere, and atmosphere. Uniformity, a basic underlying assumption of geology, states that what we see occurring now is also what we have seen in the past—the laws of nature do not change over long periods of time. Most geologic changes take place over millions of years, although there are some geologically quick disasters or catastrophes.

Modern geology is based on the theory of plate tectonics. For students to fully understand this theory, instructional time must first be spent building an understanding of the evidence supporting it— earthquake and volcano patterns, paleomagnetism, and sediment age. These studies can be done prior to an investigation of plate tectonics.

The focal point of this generalization is that landscapes, oceans, and the atmosphere go through both a natural slow process of evolution, which would be implied by laws of science, and sudden changes more connected to extraordinary and discontinuous events. Things change and these changes can be predicted and sometimes observed. In addition, there are important interactions between the solid earth, hydrosphere, atmosphere, and biosphere. Each affects the other through processes such as weathering and erosion.

Concepts Needed:
Grade 9
Sediments, sedimentation, weathering, sorting, angularity

Grade 10
Landform evolution, surface geology (erosion, weathering, transportation, streams, landforms, glaciers, earthquakes, faults), coastal processes, rates of change, topo mapping, geologic maps, mineral characteristics (hardness, color, luster, cleavage, crystal shape, composition), physiographic provinces, risks, geothermal energy

Origin and Evolution of the Earth System

INTERACTIONS AMONG ECOSYSTEMS, CONT.

Grade 11
Paleomagnetism, paleoclimates, fractional crystallization, Bowen's reaction series

Grade 12
Theory, model, scientific thought, continental drift, plate tectonics

Empirical Laws or Observed Relationships:
Evolution

Theories or Models:
Origin of Earth, gravity, crustal evolution, origin of life on Earth, origin of atmosphere, hydrosphere, geological assumptions (e.g., principle of uniformity), superposition, original horizontality, faunal succession

Learning Sequence, Grades 9–12:

Grade 9
Micro-Unit 906. At this level, students should understand how sediments are formed and connect their composition to cycles.

Micro-Unit 913. Students should create and use topographic maps.

Grade 10
Micro-Unit 1017. Students in grade 10 should examine landforms, recognizing the competitive interaction between mountain building and erosion. This involves a study of stream, coastal, glacial, and eolian features. They should identify the major physiographic provinces and, using maps and photographs, locate a variety of landforms.

Micro-Unit 1019. Students should examine faults and earthquakes in terms of stress and strain, identifying the different types of faults and their relationships to convergent and divergent plate boundaries. A study of the benefits and risks of human activities in tectonically active regions is important here. Topics should include the risks associated with large population centers and nuclear power facilities in tectonically active areas as well as the benefits of using these regions for geothermal energy sources.

Micro-Unit 1045(b). Students should understand the processes that create minerals and be able to identify a variety of common minerals by their basic characteristics.

Origin and Evolution of the Earth System

INTERACTIONS AMONG ECOSYSTEMS, CONT.

Grade 11

Micro-Unit 1107. Students at this level should understand the evidence associated with plate tectonics, how plate tectonics connect to Earth's evolution, and the effects of such changes on the evolution of life forms.

Micro-Unit 1124. Students should study how tides form and their effects on coastlines.

Micro-Unit 1137. Students can explore the relationship between rock composition and the fractional crystallization process at this point.

Grade 12

Micro-Unit 1211. Students should be aware of the history surrounding continental drift and plate tectonics so that they can better understand the development of scientific ideas and theories.

Evolution of Life, Bacteria, and Algae, and Oxygen in the Atmosphere

NSES Generalization (p. 190)

Evidence for one-celled forms of life—the bacteria—extends back more than 3.5 billion years. The evolution of life caused dramatic changes in the composition of the earth's atmosphere, which did not originally contain oxygen.

Further Description:

The origin of life is based upon the combination of elements to form amino acids, then proteins, and ultimately cells. The Miller experiments involved mixing ingredients identified as components in the early earth's atmosphere, exposing them to lightning, and forming a sludge of amino acids. This led to a series of experiments attempting to show the formation of more and more complex molecules. Eventually, through laboratory recreations of the proposed atmosphere of the early earth, proteinoids were formed. Proteinoids are round cell-like objects composed of proteins. They grow by adding to each other and dividing. Although proteinoids are not living, their formation and characteristics provided steps in the beginning of life.

Fossils provide some evidence of early life forms, although the record is scanty. Blue-green algae (stromatolites) and bacteria have been clearly identified in this early fossil record. In addition, certain rock forms such as red beds and carbonates provide evidence that the atmosphere of the early earth had very little oxygen.

Origin and Evolution of the Earth System
EVOLUTION OF LIFE AND OXYGEN IN THE ATMOSPHERE, CONT.

The process of photosynthesis carried out by some bacteria and the early algae was principally responsible for the earth's oxygen. Environmental changes, mutations possibly due to UV exposure, sexual reproduction, and the mechanism of natural selection provided for a rapid expansion of species. Life began in water but moved to land.

Evolution is supported by the fossil record, although some aspects of explanation—the theories used to account for the evolutionary process—are sometimes debated. There is no debate among competent scientists about most of the facts of evolution, only about the theories used to explain it.

Concepts Needed:
Grade 9
Types of fossils, evolution, fossilization, geologic time

Grade 10
Paleozoic, form, function, species, evolution, pre-Cambrian, Cambrian, geologic evidence (red beds, stromatolites, carbonates), lithologic, extinctions

Grade 11
Genus, species, niche, symmetry

Grade 12
Genetic mutation, autotrophs, heterotrophs, temporal evolution

Empirical Laws or Observed Relationships:
Evolution as a process, photosynthesis

Theories or Models:
Origin of life, punctuated equilibrium, natural selection, origin, evolution of hydrosphere and atmosphere

Learning Sequence, Grades 9–12:
Grade 9
Micro-Unit 934(b). Grade nine students should understand the process of photosynthesis in terms of reactants and products.

Grade 10
Micro-Unit 1006. An examination of the fossil record will introduce students to the evolutionary sequence of life forms. Of particular interest is the pre-Cambrian/Cambrian boundary, which is distinguished by a burst of life.

Origin and Evolution of the Earth System
EVOLUTION OF LIFE AND OXYGEN IN THE ATMOSPHERE, CONT.

Students should consider the extinctions of the Paleozoic era and examine their possible causes. They should examine the rapid evolution of life forms in the late Paleozoic to early Paleozoic and the effect of this rapid evolution on the atmosphere.

Micro-Unit 1007. Students should study the stages of evolution through an examination of fossils and lithologic units. Statistical analysis will help students determine how species analysis is conducted in a paleontologist manner. In this case, form and function are linked together along with environmental characteristics.

Grade 11
Micro-Unit 1102. At this grade level, students should compare fossilized remains of organisms to present-day organisms. Their similarities and differences should be noted along with their environmental preferences. Fossil keys should be used for identification purposes.

Grade 12
Micro-Unit 1209. Students should understand the biochemical basis of photosynthesis and cellular respiration and the connection of these processes to evolution. They should account for aspects of natural selection and evolution in terms of genetics and correlate the fossil evidence with other physical evidence and radioactive dating techniques.

The Origin and Evolution of the Universe

(*NSES*, p. 190)

Evidence and Theories to Explain the Evolution of the Universe

NSES Generalization (p. 190)

The origin of the universe remains one of the greatest questions in science. The "big bang" theory places the origin between 10 and 20 billion years ago, when the universe began in a hot dense state. According to this theory, the universe has been expanding ever since.

Further Description:

The big bang theory (proposed by G. Lemaitre, 1929) is supported by several pieces of evidence: (1) the Doppler shift of light from distance galaxies indicates that the speed of recession of a galaxy is proportional to the distance of the galaxy from Earth; and (2) the theory predicts that as the universe expanded and the temperature decreased, a temperature was reached at which matter and radiation no longer interacted strongly. Even today, the radiation that existed at that instant can be detected (and its measured properties—temperature, as determined by photon energy distributions, and directional distributions).

Using this theory as a model, physicists (G. Gamow, 1948) could analyze the evolution of matter. They found that the observed abundance of atoms of the different elements demonstrates trends expected for element formation in an expanding, hot, ancient fireball. Additional element formation could be explained by the formation of these heavier elements within stars.

Cosmologists, scientists who study the structure of the universe, conduct tests based on observation to determine which theories make correct predictions. Some of these tests include: (1) examining the bubblelike distribution of galaxy clusters; (2) examining red shifts; and (3) determining the mass in the universe to predict its oscillating capacity, including tabulating known matter and counting galaxies to determine if the universe is open or closed. At this time, cosmologists are not sure if the expansion will continue indefinitely.

Origin and Evolution of the Universe
EVIDENCE AND THEORIES TO EXPLAIN THE EVOLUTION OF THE UNIVERSE, CONT.

Concepts Needed:
Grade 9
Space, stars, black holes, nova, supernova

Grade 10
Models, big bang, oscillating universe, cosmology

Grade 11
EM spectrum, EM types

Grade 12
Doppler effect, radiation background (at a temperature of about 3K), density, wavelength, frequency, red shift, photon nature of light, oscillating universe

Empirical Laws or Observed Relationships:
Hubble's constant, origin of heavy elements

Theories or Models:
Big bang, special relativity (Einstein's equation for energy), general relativity (qualitative, in terms of space-time, and gravitation), conservation of angular momentum, law of universal gravitation

Learning Sequence, Grades 9–12:
Grade 9
Micro-Unit 949(e). Using star charts, students should identify actual objects in the sky, colors of stars, black holes, novas, and supernovas.

Grade 10
Micro-Unit 1046(b). Students should construct models to demonstrate varying theories of the origin of the universe. For example, a rubber band with beads glued to it could be stretched to provide a demonstration of one such theory.

Grade 11
Micro-Unit 1132. Using full electromagnetic spectrum photographs, students should view objects in the sky to see the wide range of features and information that can be used to gather astronomical data. Pictures of the sky taken using different spectrum types, such as X-rays, cosmic and radio, can be used.

Origin and Evolution of the Universe

EVIDENCE AND THEORIES TO EXPLAIN THE EVOLUTION OF THE UNIVERSE, CONT.

Grade 12

Micro-Unit 1214. Grade 12 students should use quantitative relationships like conservation of angular momentum, various laws of dynamics, Hubble's constant, Doppler shift, and spectroscopy techniques to explain the origin of the universe. They can apply much of what they have learned in physics and chemistry to this explanation.

Gravitation, Star Processes, and the Formation of the Elements

NSES Generalizations (p. 190)

Early in the history of the universe, matter, primarily the light atoms hydrogen and helium, clumped together by gravitational attraction to form countless trillions of stars. Billions of galaxies, each of which is a gravitationally bound cluster of billions of stars, now form most of the visible mass in the universe.

Stars produce energy from nuclear reactions, primarily the fusion of hydrogen to form helium. These and other processes in stars have led to the formation of all the other elements.

Further Description:

A star is an object whose energy is generated in its interior by nuclear reactions. Stars have been named using a variety of systems. Some have Arabic names (Beetlejuice); some have Greek letters, particularly those in constellations (Alpha Centauri); while others are known by English letters followed by constellation names or by catalog numbers (T Tauri).

There are nine basic properties of stars that can be measured. Through trigonometric parallax, distance of near stars can be determined. When distance is combined with brightness, luminosity can be measured. Spectra provide measures of temperature, composition, rotation, circumstellar materials, and motion. Luminosity and temperature can be used to determine the diameter of a star. By using the measures of binary stars and Kepler's laws, the mass of a star can be determined.

Due to their great magnitude, star distances are measured in light-years and parsecs. Stellar spectra provide a real key to many of the properties of stars. Both the Doppler effect and the Stefan-Boltzmann law are used in interpreting spectral data. Star brightness has been defined by apparent magnitude and absolute magnitude. These systems attempt to classify stars according to their brightness.

Origin and Evolution of the Universe

GRAVITATION, STAR PROCESSES, AND THE FORMATION OF THE ELEMENTS, CONT.

Stars come in a great variety—massive, not massive, bright, not bright. They pass through an evolutionary process. For very massive stars the end of that process is an explosion, a supernova. In addition, stars of different initial mass evolve at different rates.

Theoretical studies indicate that stars form by the contraction of an interstellar gas cloud that is so hot that atoms at the center collide at extremely high velocities. These collisions cause nuclear reactions in which hydrogen atoms are fused into helium atoms, releasing energy. A battle begins between gravity squeezing down on the star and the radiation pressure pushing out the star. As a star begins to age and run out of fuel (hydrogen), the nuclear process is modified and gravity begins to win the war.

Concepts Needed:
Grade 9
Many of these concepts can be learned at this level only in a very qualitative manner or with analogy or metaphor: white dwarf, pulsar, neutron star, blue giant, red giant, black hole, nova, supernova, stellar colors, coalescence, stellar evolution, chemical elements, luminosity, EM spectrum, emission spectroscopy, radiation pressure.

Grade 10
Star map, constellation, groups of stars, types of stars, luminosity, star distances

Grade 11
At this level, the concepts listed above should be made more quantitative, involving, when possible, terms, facts, equations, and other aspects of more advanced physics and chemistry.

Grade 12
White dwarf, pulsar, neutron star, blue giant, red giant, black hole, nova, supernova, stellar colors, coalescence, stellar evolution, chemical elements, luminosity, EM spectrum, emission spectroscopy, radiation pressure

Empirical Laws or Observed Relationships:
Inverse square law of light, Wien's law, types of stellar fusion (proton-proton, triple alpha)

Theories or Models:
Gravity, Stefan-Boltzmann law, photon theory of light, origin of elements, theory of star formation, protostar

Origin and Evolution of the Universe
GRAVITATION, STAR PROCESSES, AND THE FORMATION OF THE ELEMENTS, CONT.

Learning Sequence, Grades 9–12:

Grade 9
Micro-Unit 951. Grade nine students should understand, on a descriptive and empirical level, experiments dealing with the inverse square law of light and emission spectroscopy. For example, they should be able to interpret flame test results to identify common elements.

Grade 10
Micro-Unit 1009. Using star maps, students should identify individual stars, different types of stars, and groups of stars. They should identify constellations and visualize, through the construction of three-dimensional models, how these earth-constellation views appear.

Models will also help students visualize distances between stars. For example, if the sun is the size of a grape, the solar system would occupy a space that is the length of a football field and the next nearest star would be 100 miles away.

Micro-Unit 1037. Students should understand how intrinsic luminosity and distance affect the appearance of stars. In other words, are the stars that appear brighter in the sky only closer or are they really brighter? They can estimate the distance to visible stars using light sources on Earth.

Grade 11
Micro-Unit 1130. Students should examine stellar spectra, noting the evidence for temperature, pressure, and composition. An examination of street lights using diffraction gratings and determination of composition can lead to a meaningful study of stellar spectra.

Micro-Unit 1131. Using a data base of star characteristics, students should search for patterns and propose possible meanings of these patterns.

Grade 12
Micro-Unit 1232. At this level, students should understand the evolution of stars and be able to measure stellar translation and rotation using the Doppler effect. They should also be able to use the Stefan-Boltzmann law to calculate stellar radiation.

Part Two

Science Applications and Processes

Unifying Concepts and Processes

Science as Inquiry

Science and Technology

Science in Personal and Social Perspectives

History and Nature of Science

Unifying Concepts and Processes

NSES Standard (pp. 115–119)
As a result of activities in grades K–12, all students should develop understanding and abilities aligned with the following concepts and processes:

- *Systems, order, and organization*
- *Evidence, models, and explanation*
- *Constancy, change, and measurement*
- *Evolution and equilibrium*
- *Form and function*

Developing Student Understanding

This standard presents broad unifying concepts and processes that complement the analytic, more discipline-based perspectives presented in the other content standards. The conceptual and procedural schemes in this standard provide students with productive and insightful ways of thinking about and integrating a range of basic ideas that explain the natural and designed world.

The unifying concepts and processes in this standard are a subset of the many unifying ideas in science and technology. Some of the criteria used in the selection and organization of this standard are:

- The concepts and processes provide connections between and among traditional scientific disciplines.
- The concepts and processes are fundamental and comprehensive.
- The concepts and processes are understandable and usable by people who will implement science programs.
- The concepts and processes can be expressed and experienced in a developmentally appropriate manner during K–12 science education.

Each of the concepts and processes of this standard has a continuum of complexity that lends itself to the K–4, 5–8, and 9–12 grade-level clusters used in the other content standards. In this standard, however, the boundaries of disciplines and grade-level divisions are not distinct—teachers should develop students' understandings continuously across grades K–12.

Systems and subsystems, the nature of models, and conservation are fundamental concepts and processes included in this standard. Young students tend to interpret phenomena separately rather than in terms of a system. Force, for example, is perceived as a property of an object rather than the

Unifying Concepts and Processes

result of interacting bodies. Students do not recognize the differences between parts and whole systems, but view them as similar. Therefore, teachers of science need to help students recognize the properties of objects, as emphasized in grade-level content standards, while helping them to understand systems.

As another example, students in middle school and high school view models as physical copies of reality and not as conceptual representations. Teachers should help students understand that models are developed and tested by comparing the model with observations of reality.

Teachers in elementary grades should recognize that students' reports of changes in such things as volume, mass, and space can represent errors common to well-recognized developmental stages of children.

Guide to the Content Standard

Some of the fundamental concepts that underlie this standard are:

Systems, Order, and Organization. The natural and designed world is complex; it is too large and complicated to investigate and comprehend all at once. Scientists and students learn to define small portions for the convenience of investigation. The units of investigation can be referred to as "systems." A system is an organized group of related objects or components that form a whole. Systems can consist, for example, of organisms, machines, fundamental particles, galaxies, ideas, numbers, transportation, and education. Systems have boundaries, components, resources flow (input and output), and feedback.

The goal of this standard is to think and analyze in terms of systems. Thinking and analyzing in terms of systems will help students keep track of mass, energy, objects, organisms, and events referred to in the other content standards. The idea of simple systems encompasses subsystems as well as identifying the structure and function of systems, feedback and equilibrium, and the distinction between open and closed systems.

Science assumes that the behavior of the universe is not capricious, that nature is the same everywhere, and that it is understandable and predictable. Students can develop an understanding of regularities in systems, and by extension, the universe; they then can develop understanding of basic laws, theories, and models that explain the world.

Newton's laws of force and motion, Kepler's laws of planetary motion, conservation laws, Darwin's laws of natural selection, and chaos theory all

Unifying Concepts and Processes

exemplify the idea of order and regularity. An assumption of order establishes the basis for cause-effect relationships and predictability.

Prediction is the use of knowledge to identify and explain observations, or changes, in advance. The use of mathematics, especially probability, allows for greater or lesser certainty of predictions.

Order—the behavior of units of matter, objects, organisms, or events in the universe—can be described statistically. Probability is the relative certainty (or uncertainty) that individuals can assign to selected events happening (or not happening) in a specified space or time. In science, reduction of uncertainty occurs through such processes as the development of knowledge about factors influencing objects, organisms, systems, or events; better and more observations; and better explanatory models.

Types and levels of organization provide useful ways of thinking about the world. Types of organization include the periodic table of elements and the classification of organisms. Physical systems can be described at different levels of organization—such as fundamental particles, atoms, and molecules. Living systems also have different levels of organization—for example, cells, tissues, organs, organisms, populations, and communities. The complexity and number of fundamental units change in extended hierarchies of organization. Within these systems, interactions between components occur. Further, systems at different levels of organization can manifest different properties and functions.

Evidence, Models, and Explanation. Evidence consists of observations and data on which to base scientific explanations. Using evidence to understand interactions allows individuals to predict changes in natural and designed systems.

Models are tentative schemes or structures that correspond to real objects, events, or classes of events, and that have explanatory power. Models help scientists and engineers understand how things work. Models take many forms, including physical objects, plans, mental constructs, mathematical equations, and computer simulations.

Scientific explanations incorporate existing scientific knowledge and new evidence from observations, experiments, or models into internally consistent, logical statements. Different terms, such as "hypothesis," "model," "law," "principle," "theory," and "paradigm" are used to describe various types of scientific explanations. As students develop and as they understand more science concepts and processes, their explanations should become more

Unifying Concepts and Processes

sophisticated. That is, their scientific explanations should more frequently include a rich scientific knowledge base, evidence of logic, higher levels of analysis, greater tolerance of criticism and uncertainty, and a clearer demonstration of the relationship between logic, evidence, and current knowledge.

Constancy, Change, and Measurement. Although most things are in the process of becoming different—changing—some properties of objects and processes are characterized by constancy, including the speed of light, the charge of an electron, and the total mass plus energy in the universe. Changes might occur, for example, in properties of materials, position of objects, motion, and form and function of systems. Interactions within and among systems result in change. Changes vary in rate, scale, and pattern, including trends and cycles.

Energy can be transferred and matter can be changed. Nevertheless, when measured, the sum of energy and matter in systems, and by extension in the universe, remains the same. Changes in systems can be quantified. Evidence for interactions and subsequent change and the formulation of scientific explanations are often clarified through quantitative distinctions—measurement. Mathematics is essential for accurately measuring change.

Different systems of measurement are used for different purposes. Scientists usually use the metric system. An important part of measurement is knowing when to use which system. For example, a meteorologist might use degrees Fahrenheit when reporting the weather to the public, but in writing scientific reports, the meteorologist would use degrees Celsius.

Scale includes understanding that different characteristics, properties, or relationships within a system might change as its dimensions are increased or decreased.

Rate involves comparing one measured quantity with another measured quantity, for example, 60 meters per second. Rate is also a measure of change for a part relative to the whole, for example, change in birth rate as part of population growth.

Evolution and Equilibrium. Evolution is a series of changes, some gradual and some sporadic, that accounts for the present form and function of objects, organisms, and natural and designed systems. The general idea of evolution is that the present arises from materials and forms of the past. Although evolution is most commonly associated with the biological theory

Unifying Concepts and Processes

explaining the process of descent with modification of organisms from common ancestors, evolution also describes changes in the universe.

Equilibrium is a physical state in which forces and changes occur in opposite and offsetting directions: for example, opposite forces are of the same magnitude, or offsetting changes occur at equal rates. Steady state, balance, and homeostasis also describe equilibrium states. Interacting units of matter tend toward equilibrium states in which the energy is distributed as randomly and uniformly as possible.

Form and Function. Form and function are complementary aspects of objects, organisms, and systems in the natural and designed world. The form or shape of an object or system is frequently related to use, operation, or function. Function frequently relies on form. Understanding of form and function applies to different levels of organization. Students should be able to explain function by referring to form and explain form by referring to function.

Science as Inquiry

NSES Content Standard A (pp. 173–176)
As a result of activities in grades 9–12, all students should develop
* *Abilities necessary to do scientific inquiry*
* *Understandings about scientific inquiry*

Developing Student Abilities and Understanding

For students to develop the abilities that characterize science as inquiry, they must actively participate in scientific investigations, and they must actually use the cognitive and manipulative skills associated with the formulation of scientific explanations. This standard describes the fundamental abilities and understandings of inquiry, as well as a larger framework for conducting scientific investigations of natural phenomena.

In grades 9–12, students should develop sophistication in their abilities and understanding of scientific inquiry. Students can understand that experiments are guided by concepts and are performed to test ideas. Some students still have trouble with variables and controlled experiments. Further, students often have trouble dealing with data that seem anomalous and in proposing explanations based on evidence and logic rather than on their prior beliefs about the natural world.

One challenge to teachers of science and to curriculum developers is making science investigations meaningful. Investigations should derive from questions and issues that have meaning for students. Scientific topics that have been highlighted by current events provide one source, whereas actual science- and technology-related problems provide another source of meaningful investigations. Finally, teachers of science should remember that some experiences begin with little meaning for students but develop meaning through active involvement, continued exposure, and growing skill and understanding.

A critical component of successful scientific inquiry in grades 9–12 includes having students reflect on the concepts that guide the inquiry. Also important is the prior establishment of an adequate knowledge base to support the investigation and help develop scientific explanations. The concepts of the world that students bring to school will shape the way they engage in science investigations, and serve as filters for their explanations of scientific phenomena. Left unexamined, the limited nature of students' beliefs will interfere with their ability to develop a deep understanding of science. Thus, in a full inquiry, instructional strategies such as small-group discussions, labeled

Science as Inquiry

drawings, writings, and concept mapping should be used by the teacher of science to gain information about students' current explanations. Those student explanations then become a baseline for instruction as teachers help students construct explanations aligned with scientific knowledge; teachers also help students evaluate their own explanations and those made by scientists.

Students also need to learn how to analyze evidence and data. The evidence they analyze may be from their investigations, other students' investigations, or databases. Data manipulation and analysis strategies need to be modeled by teachers of science and practiced by students. Determining the range of the data, the mean and mode values of the data, plotting the data, developing mathematical functions from the data, and looking for anomalous data are all examples of analyses students can perform. Teachers of science can ask questions, such as "What explanation did you expect to develop from the data?" "Were there any surprises in the data?" "How confident do you feel about the accuracy of the data?" Students should answer questions such as these during full and partial inquiries.

Public discussions of the explanations proposed by students is a form of peer review of investigations, and peer review is an important aspect of science. Talking with peers about science experiences helps students develop meaning and understanding. Their conversations clarify the concepts and processes of science, helping students make sense of the content of science. Teachers of science should engage students in conversations that focus on questions, such as "How do we know?" "How certain are you of those results?" "Is there a better way to do the investigation?" "If you had to explain this to someone who knew nothing about the project, how would you do it?" "Is there an alternative scientific explanation for the one we proposed?" "Should we do the investigation over?" "Do we need more evidence?" "What are our sources of experimental error?" "How do you account for an explanation that is different from ours?"

Questions like these make it possible for students to analyze data, develop a richer knowledge base, reason using science concepts, make connections between evidence and explanations, and recognize alternative explanations. Ideas should be examined and discussed in class so that other students can benefit from the feedback. Teachers of science can use the ideas of students in their class, ideas from other classes, and ideas from texts, databases, or other sources—but scientific ideas and methods should be discussed in the fashion just described.

Science as Inquiry

Guide to the Content Standard
Fundamental abilities and concepts that underlie this standard include:

Abilities Necessary to Do Scientific Inquiry

Identify Questions and Concepts That Guide Scientific Investigations. Students should formulate a testable hypothesis and demonstrate the logical connections between the scientific concepts guiding a hypothesis and the design of an experiment. They should demonstrate appropriate procedures, a knowledge base, and conceptual understanding of scientific investigations.

Design and Conduct Scientific Investigations. Designing and conducting a scientific investigation requires introduction to the major concepts in the area being investigated, proper equipment, safety precautions, assistance with methodological problems, recommendations for use of technologies, clarification of ideas that guide the inquiry, and scientific knowledge obtained from sources other than the actual investigation. The investigation may also require student clarification of the question, method, controls, and variables; student organization and display of data; student revision of methods and explanations; and a public presentation of the results with a critical response from peers. Regardless of the scientific investigation performed, students must use evidence, apply logic, and construct an argument for their proposed explanations.

Use Technology and Mathematics to Improve Investigations and Communications. A variety of technologies, such as hand tools, measuring instruments, and calculators, should be an integral component of scientific investigations. The use of computers for the collection, analysis, and display of data is also a part of this standard. Mathematics plays an essential role in all aspects of an inquiry. For example, measurement is used for posing questions, formulas are used for developing explanations, and charts and graphs are used for communicating results.

Formulate and Revise Scientific Explanations and Models Using Logic and Evidence. Student inquiries should culminate in formulating an explanation or model. Models should be physical, conceptual, and mathematical. In the process of answering the questions, the students should engage in

Science as Inquiry

discussions and arguments that result in the revision of their explanations. These discussions should be based on scientific knowledge, the use of logic, and evidence from their investigation.

Recognize and Analyze Alternative Explanations and Models. This aspect of the standard emphasizes the critical abilities of analyzing an argument by reviewing current scientific understanding, weighing the evidence, and examining the logic so as to decide which explanations and models are best. In other words, although there may be several plausible explanations, they do not all have equal weight. Students should be able to use scientific criteria to find the preferred explanations.

Communicate and Defend a Scientific Argument. Students in school science programs should develop the abilities associated with accurate and effective communication. These include writing and following procedures, expressing concepts, reviewing information, summarizing data, using language appropriately, developing diagrams and charts, explaining statistical analysis, speaking clearly and logically, constructing a reasoned argument, and responding appropriately to critical comments.

Understandings About Scientific Inquiry

- Scientists usually inquire about how physical, living, or designed systems function. Conceptual principles and knowledge guide scientific inquiries. Historical and current scientific knowledge influence the design and interpretation of investigations and the evaluation of proposed explanations made by other scientists.

- Scientists conduct investigations for a wide variety of reasons. For example, they may wish to discover new aspects of the natural world, explain recently observed phenomena, or test the conclusions of prior investigations or the predictions of current theories.

- Scientists rely on technology to enhance the gathering and manipulation of data. New techniques and tools provide new evidence to guide inquiry and new methods to gather data, thereby contributing to the advance of science. The accuracy and precision of the data, and therefore the quality of the exploration, depends on the technology used.

- Mathematics is essential in scientific inquiry. Mathematical tools and models guide and improve the posing of questions, gathering data, constructing explanations and communicating results.

Science as Inquiry

- Scientific explanations must adhere to criteria such as: a proposed explanation must be logically consistent; it must abide by the rules of evidence; it must be open to questions and possible modification; and it must be based on historical and current scientific knowledge.
- Results of scientific inquiry—new knowledge and methods—emerge from different types of investigations and public communication among scientists. In communicating and defending the results of scientific inquiry, arguments must be logical and demonstrate connections between natural phenomena, investigations, and the historical body of scientific knowledge. In addition, the methods and procedures that scientists used to obtain evidence must be clearly reported to enhance opportunities for further investigation.

Science as Technology

NSES Content Standard E (pp. 190–193)
As a result of activities in grades 9–12, all students should develop
* *Abilities of technological design*
* *Understandings about science and technology*

Developing Student Abilities and Understanding

This standard has two equally important parts—developing students' abilities of technological design and developing students' understanding about science and technology. Although these are science education standards, the relationship between science and technology is so close that any presentation of science without developing an understanding of technology would portray an inaccurate picture of science.

In the course of solving any problem where students try to meet certain criteria within constraints, they will find that the ideas and methods of science that they know, or can learn, can be powerful aids. Students also find that they need to call on other sources of knowledge and skill, such as cost, risk, and benefit analysis, and aspects of critical thinking and creativity. Learning experiences associated with this standard should include examples of technological achievement in which science has played a part and examples where technological advances contributed directly to scientific progress.

Students can understand and use the design model outlined in this standard. Students respond positively to the concrete, practical, outcome orientation of design problems before they are able to engage in the abstract, theoretical nature of many scientific inquiries. In general, high school students do not distinguish between the roles of science and technology. Helping them do so is implied by this standard. This lack of distinction between science and technology is further confused by students' positive perceptions of science, as when they associate it with medical research and use the common phrase "scientific progress." However, their association of technology is often with environmental problems and another common phrase, "technological problems." With regard to the connection between science and technology, students as well as many adults and teachers of science indicate a belief that science influences technology. This belief is captured by the common and only partially accurate definition "technology is applied science." Few students understand that technology influences science. Unraveling these misconceptions of science and technology and developing accurate concepts of the role, place, limits, possibilities and relationships of science and technology is the challenge of this standard.

Science as Technology

The choice of design tasks and related learning activities is an important and difficult part of addressing this standard. In choosing technological learning activities, teachers of science will have to bear in mind some important issues. For example, whether to involve students in a full or partial design problem; or whether to engage them in meeting a need through technology or in studying the technological work of others. Another issue is how to select a task that brings out the various ways in which science and technology interact, providing a basis for reflection on the nature of technology while learning the science concepts involved.

In grades 9–12, design tasks should explore a range of contexts including both those immediately familiar in the homes, school, and community of the students and those from wider regional, national, or global contexts. The tasks should promote different ways to tackle the problems so that different design solutions can be implemented by different students. Successful completion of design problems requires that the students meet criteria while addressing conflicting constraints. Where constructions are involved, these might draw on technical skills and understandings developed within the science program, technical and craft skills developed in other school work, or require developing new skills.

Over the high school years, the tasks should cover a range of needs, of materials, and of different aspects of science. For example, a suitable design problem could include assembling electronic components to control a sequence of operations or analyzing the features of different athletic shoes to see the criteria and constraints imposed by the sport, human anatomy, and materials. Some tasks should involve science ideas drawn from more than one field of science. These can be complex, for example, a machine that incorporates both mechanical and electrical control systems.

Although some experiences in science and technology will emphasize solving problems and meeting needs by focusing on products, experience also should include problems about system design, cost, risk, benefit, and very importantly, trade-offs.

Because this study of technology occurs within science courses, the number of these activities must be limited. Details specified in this standard are criteria to ensure quality and balance in a small number of tasks and are not meant to require a large number of such activities. Many abilities and understandings of this standard can be developed as part of activities designed for other content standards.

Science as Technology

Guide to the Content Standard
Fundamental abilities and concepts that underlie this standard include:

Abilities of Technological Design

Identify a Problem or Design an Opportunity. Students should be able to identify new problems or needs and to change and improve current technological designs.

Propose Designs and Choose Between Alternative Solutions. Students should demonstrate thoughtful planning for a piece of technology or technique. Students should be introduced to the roles of models and simulations in these processes.

Implement a Proposed Solution. A variety of skills can be needed in proposing a solution depending on the type of technology that is involved. The construction of artifacts can require the skills of cutting, shaping, treating, and joining common materials—such as wood, metal, plastics, and textiles. Solutions can also be implemented using computer software.

Evaluate the Solution and Its Consequences. Students should test any solution against the needs and criteria it was designed to meet. At this stage, new criteria not originally considered may be reviewed.

Communicate the Problem, Process, and Solution. Students should present their results to students, teachers, and others in a variety of ways, such as orally, in writing, and in other forms—including models, diagrams, and demonstrations.

Understandings About Science and Technology
- Scientists in different disciplines ask different questions, use different methods of investigation, and accept different types of evidence to support their explanations. Many scientific investigations require the contributions of individuals from different disciplines, including engineering. New disciplines of science, such as geophysics and biochemistry often emerge at the interface of two older disciplines.
- Science often advances with the introduction of new technologies. Solving technological problems often results in new scientific knowledge. New

Science as Technology

technologies often extend the current levels of scientific understanding and introduce new areas of research.
- Creativity, imagination, and a good knowledge base are all required in the work of science and engineering.
- Science and technology are pursued for different purposes. Scientific inquiry is driven by the desire to understand the natural world, and technological design is driven by the need to meet human needs and solve human problems. Technology, by its nature, has a more direct effect on society than science because its purpose is to solve human problems, help humans adapt, and fulfill human aspirations. Technological solutions may create new problems. Science, by its nature, answers questions that may or may not directly influence humans. Sometimes scientific advances challenge people's beliefs and practical explanations concerning various aspects of the world.
- Technological knowledge is often not made public because of patents and the financial potential of the idea or invention. Scientific knowledge is made public through presentations at professional meetings and publications in scientific journals.

Science in Personal and Social Perspectives

NSES Content Standard F (pp. 193–199)
As a result of activities in grades 9–12, all students should develop understanding of:

- *Personal and community health*
- *Population growth*
- *Natural resources*
- *Environmental quality*
- *Natural and human-induced hazards*
- *Science and technology in local, national, and global challenges*

Developing Student Understanding

The organizing principles for this standard do not identify specific personal and societal challenges; rather they form a set of conceptual organizers, fundamental understandings, and implied actions for most contemporary issues. The organizing principles apply to local as well as global phenomena and represent challenges that occur on scales that vary from quite short—for example, natural hazards—to very long—for example, the potential result of global changes.

By grades 9–12, many students have a fairly sound understanding of the overall functioning of some human systems, such as the digestive, respiratory, and circulatory systems. They might not have a clear understanding of others, such as the human nervous, endocrine, and immune systems. Therefore, students may have difficulty with specific mechanisms and processes related to health issues.

Most high school students have a concept of populations of organisms, but they have a poorly developed understanding of the relationships among populations within a community and connections between populations and other ideas such as competition for resources. Few students understand and apply the idea of interdependence when considering interactions among populations, environments, and resources. If, for example, students are asked about the size of populations and why some populations would be larger, they often simply describe rather than reason about interdependence or energy flow.

Students may exhibit a general idea of cycling matter in ecosystems, but they may center on short chains of the cyclical process and express the misconception that matter is created and destroyed at each step of the cycle

Science in Personal and Social Perspectives

rather than undergoing continuous transformation. Instruction using charts of the flow of matter through an ecosystem and emphasizing the reasoning involved with the entire process may enable students to develop more accurate conceptions.

Many high-school students hold the view that science should inform society about various issues and society should set policy about what research is important. In general, students have rather simple and naive ideas about the interactions between science and society. There is some research supporting the idea that S-T-S (science, technology, and society) curriculum helps improve student understanding of various aspects of science- and technology-related societal challenges.

Guide to the Content Standard
Fundamental concepts and principles that underlie this standard include

Personal and Community Health
- Hazards and the potential for accidents exist. Regardless of the environment, the possibility of injury, illness, disability, or death may be present. Humans have a variety of mechanisms—sensory, motor, emotional, social, and technological— that can reduce and modify hazards.

- The severity of disease symptoms is dependent on many factors, such as human resistance and the virulence of the disease-producing organism. Many diseases can be prevented, controlled, or cured. Some diseases, such as cancer, result from specific body dysfunctions and cannot be transmitted.

- Personal choice concerning fitness and health involves multiple factors. Personal goals, peer and social pressures, ethnic and religious beliefs, and understanding of biological consequences can all influence decisions about health practices.

- An individual's mood and behavior may be modified by substances. The modification may be beneficial or detrimental depending on the motives, type of substance, duration of use, pattern of use, level of influence, and short- and long-term effects. Students should understand that drugs can result in physical dependence and can increase the risk of injury, accidents, and death.

Science in Personal and Social Perspectives

- Selection of foods and eating patterns determine nutritional balance. Nutritional balance has a direct effect on growth and development and personal well-being. Personal and social factors— such as habits, family income, ethnic heritage, body size, advertising, and peer pressure—influence nutritional choices.

- Families serve basic health needs, especially for young children. Regardless of the family structure, individuals have families that involve a variety of physical, mental, and social relationships that influence the maintenance and improvement of health.

- Sexuality is basic to the physical, mental, and social development of humans. Students should understand that human sexuality involves biological functions, psychological motives, and cultural, ethnic, religious, and technological influences. Sex is a basic and powerful force that has consequences to individuals' health and to society. Students should understand various methods of controlling the reproduction process and that each method has a different type of effectiveness and different health and social consequences.

Population Growth

- Populations grow or decline through the combined effects of births and deaths, and through emigration and immigration. Populations can increase through linear or exponential growth, with effects on resource use and environmental pollution.

- Various factors influence birth rates and fertility rates, such as average levels of affluence and education, importance of children in the labor force, education and employment of women, infant mortality rates, costs of raising children, availability and reliability of birth control methods, and religious beliefs and cultural norms that influence personal decisions about family size.

- Populations can reach limits to growth. Carrying capacity is the maximum number of individuals that can be supported in a given environment. The limitation is not the availability of space, but the number of people in relation to resources and the capacity of earth systems to support human beings. Changes in technology can cause significant changes, either positive or negative, in carrying capacity.

Science in Personal and Social Perspectives

Natural Resources

- Human populations use resources in the environment in order to maintain and improve their existence. Natural resources have been and will continue to be used to maintain human populations.

- The earth does not have infinite resources; increasing human consumption places severe stress on the natural processes that renew some resources, and it depletes those resources that cannot be renewed.

- Humans use many natural systems as resources. Natural systems have the capacity to reuse waste, but that capacity is limited. Natural systems can change to an extent that exceeds the limits of organisms to adapt naturally or humans to adapt technologically.

Environmental Quality

- Natural ecosystems provide an array of basic processes that affect humans. Those processes include maintenance of the quality of the atmosphere, generation of soils, control of the hydrologic cycle, disposal of wastes, and recycling of nutrients. Humans are changing many of these basic processes, and the changes may be detrimental to humans.

- Materials from human societies affect both physical and chemical cycles of the earth.

- Many factors influence environmental quality. Factors that students might investigate include population growth, resource use, population distribution, overconsumption, the capacity of technology to solve problems, poverty, the role of economic, political, and religious views, and different ways humans view the earth.

Natural and Human-Induced Hazards

- Normal adjustments of earth may be hazardous for humans. Humans live at the interface between the atmosphere driven by solar energy and the upper mantle where convection creates changes in the earth's solid crust. As societies have grown, become stable, and come to value aspects of the environment, vulnerability to natural processes of change has increased.

- Human activities can enhance potential for hazards. Acquisition of resources, urban growth, and waste disposal can accelerate rates of natural change.

Science in Personal and Social Perspectives

- Some hazards, such as earthquakes, volcanic eruptions, and severe weather, are rapid and spectacular. But there are slow and progressive changes that also result in problems for individuals and societies. For example, change in stream channel position, erosion of bridge foundations, sedimentation in lakes and harbors, coastal erosions, and continuing erosion and wasting of soil and landscapes can all negatively affect society.

- Natural and human-induced hazards present the need for humans to assess potential danger and risk. Many changes in the environment designed by humans bring benefits to society, as well as cause risks. Students should understand the costs and trade-offs of various hazards—ranging from those with minor risk to a few people to major catastrophes with major risk to many people. The scale of events and the accuracy with which scientists and engineers can (and cannot) predict events are important considerations.

Science and Technology in Local, National, and Global Challenges

- Science and technology are essential social enterprises, but alone they can only indicate what can happen, not what should happen. The latter involves human decisions about the use of knowledge.

- Understanding basic concepts and principles of science and technology should precede active debate about the economics, policies, politics, and ethics of various science- and technology-related challenges. However, understanding science alone will not resolve local, national, or global challenges.

- Progress in science and technology can be affected by social issues and challenges. Funding priorities for specific health problems serve as examples of ways that social issues influence science and technology.

- Individuals and society must decide on proposals involving new research and the introduction of new technologies into society. Decisions involve assessment of alternatives, risks, costs, and benefits and consideration of who benefits and who suffers, who pays and gains, and what the risks are and who bears them. Students should understand the appropriateness and value of basic questions— "What can happen?"— "What are the odds?"— and "How do scientists and engineers know what will happen?"

- Humans have a major effect on other species. For example, the influence of humans on other organisms occurs through land use—which decreases space available to other species—and pollution—which changes the chemical composition of air, soil, and water.

History and Nature of Science

***NSES*, Content Standard G** (pp. 200–204)
As a result of activities in grades 9–12, all students should develop understanding of:

- *Science as a human endeavor*
- *Nature of scientific knowledge*
- *Historical perspectives*

Developing Student Understanding

The *National Science Education Standards* use history to elaborate various aspects of scientific inquiry, the nature of science, and science in different historical and cultural perspectives. The standards on the history and nature of science are closely aligned with the nature of science and historical episodes described in the American Association for the Advancement of Science *Benchmarks for Science Literacy*. Teachers of science can incorporate other historical examples that may accommodate different interests, topics, disciplines, and cultures—as the intention of the standard is to develop an understanding of the human dimensions of science, the nature of scientific knowledge, and the enterprise of science in society—and not to develop a comprehensive understanding of history.

Little research has been reported on the use of history in teaching about the nature of science. But learning about the history of science might help students to improve their general understanding of science. Teachers should be sensitive to the students' lack of knowledge and perspective on time, duration, and succession when it comes to historical study. High school students may have difficulties understanding the views of historical figures. For example, students may think of historical figures as inferior because they did not understand what we do today. This "Whiggish perspective" seems to hold for some students with regard to scientists whose theories have been displaced.

Guide to the Content Standard
Fundamental concepts and principles that underlie this standard include

Science as a Human Endeavor
- Individuals and teams have contributed and will continue to contribute to the scientific enterprise. Doing science or engineering can be as simple as

History and Nature of Science

an individual conducting field studies or as complex as hundreds of people working on a major scientific question or technological problem. Pursuing science as a career or as a hobby can be both fascinating and intellectually rewarding.
- Scientists have ethical traditions. Scientists value peer review, truthful reporting about the methods and outcomes of investigations, and making public the results of work. Violations of such norms do occur, but scientists responsible for such violations are censured by their peers.
- Scientists are influenced by societal, cultural, and personal beliefs and ways of viewing the world. Science is not separate from society but rather science is a part of society.

Nature of Scientific Knowledge
- Science distinguishes itself from other ways of knowing and from other bodies of knowledge through the use of empirical standards, logical arguments, and skepticism, as scientists strive for the best possible explanations about the natural world.

- Scientific explanations must meet certain criteria. First and foremost, they must be consistent with experimental and observational evidence about nature, and must make accurate predictions, when appropriate, about systems being studied. They should also be logical, respect the rules of evidence, be open to criticism, report methods and procedures, and make knowledge public. Explanations on how the natural world changes based on myths, personal beliefs, religious values, mystical inspiration, superstition, or authority may be personally useful and socially relevant, but they are not scientific.

- Because all scientific ideas depend on experimental and observational confirmation, all scientific knowledge is, in principle, subject to change as new evidence becomes available. The core ideas of science such as the conservation of energy or the laws of motion have been subjected to a wide variety of confirmations and are therefore unlikely to change in the areas in which they have been tested. In areas where data or understanding are incomplete, such as the details of human evolution or questions surrounding global warming, new data may well lead to changes in current ideas or resolve current conflicts. In situations where information is still fragmentary, it is normal for scientific ideas to be incomplete, but this is also where the opportunity for making advances may be greatest.

History and Nature of Science

Historical Perspectives

- In history, diverse cultures have contributed scientific knowledge and technologic inventions. Modern science began to evolve rapidly in Europe several hundred years ago. During the past two centuries, it has contributed significantly to the industrialization of Western and non-Western cultures. However, other, non-European cultures have developed scientific ideas and solved human problems through technology.

- Usually, changes in science occur as small modifications in extant knowledge. The daily work of science and engineering results in incremental advances in our understanding of the world and our ability to meet human needs and aspirations. Much can be learned about the internal workings of science and the nature of science from study of individual scientists, their daily work, and their efforts to advance scientific knowledge in their area of study.

- Occasionally there are advances in science and technology that have important and long-lasting effects on science and society. Examples of such advances include the following:

    Copernican revolution
    Newtonian mechanics
    Relativity
    Geologic time scale
    Plate Tectonics
    Atomic theory
    Nuclear physics
    Biological evolution
    Germ theory
    Industrial revolution
    Molecular biology
    Information and communication
    Quantum theory
    Galactic universe
    Medical and health technology

- The historical perspective of scientific explanations demonstrates how scientific knowledge changes by evolving over time, almost always building on earlier knowledge.

Appendix A

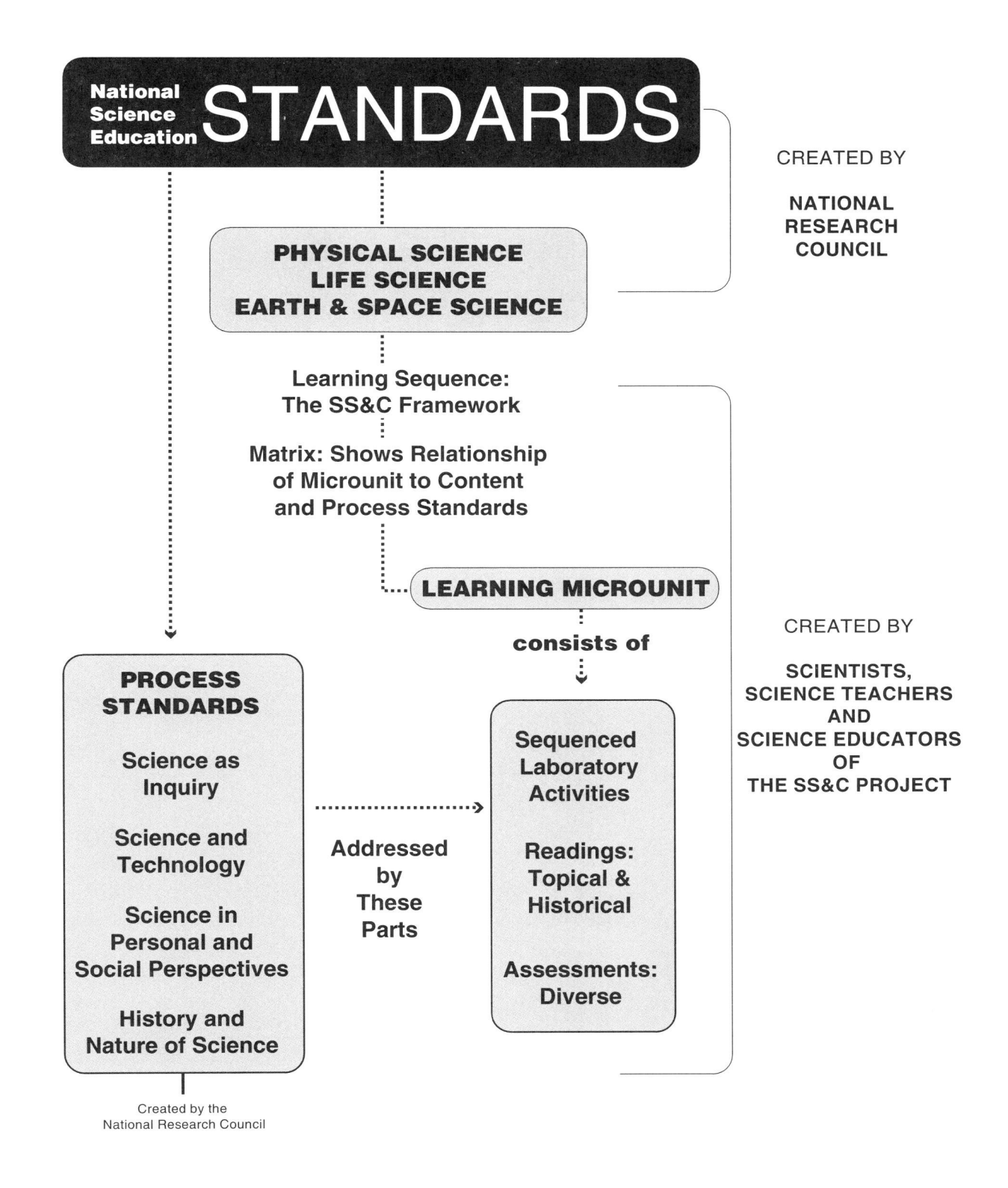

National Science Education STANDARDS

CREATED BY

NATIONAL RESEARCH COUNCIL

PHYSICAL SCIENCE
LIFE SCIENCE
EARTH & SPACE SCIENCE

Learning Sequence:
The SS&C Framework

Matrix: Shows Relationship
of Microunit to Content
and Process Standards

LEARNING MICROUNIT

consists of

CREATED BY

**SCIENTISTS,
SCIENCE TEACHERS
AND
SCIENCE EDUCATORS
OF
THE SS&C PROJECT**

PROCESS STANDARDS

Science as Inquiry

Science and Technology

Science in Personal and Social Perspectives

History and Nature of Science

Created by the National Research Council

Addressed by These Parts

Sequenced Laboratory Activities

Readings: Topical & Historical

Assessments: Diverse

Appendix B

Sample Page from SS&C Matrix

This is a good opportunity to build an empirical base for subsequent theoretical work. At this level some kinetic theory can be developed descriptively and qualitatively, leading students to understand how gases exert pressures, how temperature increases change the volume or pressure of a gas under various constraints, etc. The concept of atoms and molecules can be developed as they relate to vibrations and random motion.

Physics (*Framework,* page 34, learning sequence-grade 9, para. 1)

Science as Inquiry	Science and Technology	Science in Personal and Social Perspectives	History and Nature of Science
Formulate and revise explanation; analyze alternative explanations. Descartes' Rules of Inquiry (G, pp. 204–205) Antoine Arnauld on Method in Scientific Investigation (G, pp. 205–210)	What should scuba divers know about the gas law? (CH, pp. 4–6) How do they steer hot air balloons? (SU, pp. 94–95 and RO, pp. 100–101) How do they get the foam into a can of shaving cream? (SU, pp. 127)	How do they get natural gas into homes? (SU, p. 148)	Galileo, on the effect of a vacuum (G, p. 124) Torricelli on the weight of the atmosphere (G, p. 126) Some experiments of the Academia del Cimento-mercury barometer (G, p. 127) 1699—Amontons, volume increased at a steady rate as the temperature increased: gas volume and temperature (AS, p. 177) 1662—Boyle's law; Robert Hooke builds an improved air pump (AS, p. 155)

Appendix C

Basic Tenets of Scope, Sequence, and Coordination

1. To provide science learning in four subject areas each year: biology, chemistry, physics, and the earth and space sciences;

2. To explicitly take into account students' prior knowledge and experience, as expressed in their preconceptions and metaphors (much of this is available in the literature);

3. To provide a sequence of content, and the learning of it, from concrete experience and descriptive expression to abstract symbolism and quantitative expression;

4. To provide concrete experiences with science phenomena before the use of terminology that describes or represents those phenomena;

5. To revisit concepts, principles, and theories at successively higher levels of abstraction;

6. To coordinate the four science subjects so as to interrelate basic concepts and principles;

7. To utilize the short-term motivational power of relevance by connecting the science learned to subject areas outside of science (such as history, art, and music), to the practical applications of how devices in our technology work, and to the challenge of solving those personal and societal problems that have relevant underlying scientific components;

8. To utilize the long-term motivational power of sudden and profound understandings of science and of the awe that stems from comprehension of the power and universality of a relatively small number of fundamental principles of science;

9. To greatly reduce topical coverage, with an increased emphasis on greater depth of understanding of those fewer fundamental topics; and

10. To create assessment methods, items, and instruments to measure student skills, knowledge, understandings, and attitudes, both for program evaluation and the requirement of assigning grades, which are fully consistent with tenets 1–9.

Glossary

Scientific or Technical *Fact* or *Term*. A *term* is an agreed upon name of an entity, object, specific event or time period, classification category, organism, or part of an organism. Because of their specificity, terms are almost always unique to a particular science or technical field or subfield. Terms are used to assure precision of communication and are generally learned as needed in reading science or using the terms in verbal or written communications about science. *Facts* include measurements or observations that can be consistently replicated and are most often found in reference handbooks. Facts also include operational definitions of basic quantities like mass, length, or time, or the conversion among such quantities.

Scientific *Concept*. A mental construct formed from sensory perceptions of a regularly occurring natural phenomenon, or such observations of a property or characteristic of matter, which is observed or detected in several different contexts, and which scientists agree to represent with a word or words, but also with other symbols, many of which are mathematical symbols. Some representations of science concepts are derived from others (i.e., speed derived from concepts of distance and time). When a derived science concept is in the form of an equation, it is a mathematical definition, not a natural relationship (e.g., mass density).

ature *Empirical Law* or *Observed Relationship*. A generalization of a relationship that has, through observation or measurement, been established among the phenomena represented by two or more concepts (with proper controls when there are more than two variables), but which relies on no theory or model for its expression or utilization (e.g., Snell's law of refraction; Boyle's law, pressure of a gas as a function of volume, holding temperature and number of moles of the gas constant). An empirical law is often a precursor to a theory, and such laws in their most primitive form are often regarded as theories (e.g., Newton's "theory of colours," a precursor to the wave model and to the electromagnetic theory; the empirical law of evolution, in contrast to the theory of natural selection).

Scientific *Theory* or *Model*. A *model* is a representation, usually visual but sometimes mathematical, used to aid in the description or understanding of a scientific phenomenon, theory, empirical law,

Glossary

physical entity, organism, or part of an organism (e.g., wave model, particle model, greenhouse model of Earth and its atmosphere). A *theory* is used to explain facts, observations, phenomena, and empirical laws. A theory is expressed in terms of various concepts that often have been quantified and for which symbols are used in their representation. Thus such theories are often mathematical. In its simplest form a theory provides hypotheses by which it can be tested. All theories are tentative, and even the most recent version of one of them is merely one stage in a continuous process. Theories are unlike the facts, observations, and empirical laws of science, all of which can be replicated and are independent of the observer and therefore map one-to-one with physical reality. Different theorists can create quite different theories, and these alternative theories *can* explain the *same* set of phenomena. To the degree that such theories make the same predictions, they are equally valid. In that sense, the theories are not reflections of reality and may well be considered subjective. Scientists accept as the best theories or models those that make the most comprehensive, testable predictions.

The fact that a theory makes a prediction, and that prediction often results in a new empirical law, merely *corroborates* the theory. The theory is never proved. But the resulting empirical law stands until such time that replication fails to produce the same result or results.

Theories, more than any other expression in science, can be described at many different levels of abstraction, from simple word explanations to complex mathematical equations.

Application of Science. Utilization of scientific observations, facts, empirical laws, or confirmed predictions of theories to design or create a functional device (called *technology*) or to produce a phenomenon for practical or aesthetic reasons, which may not exist or occur in the natural world (e.g., applications of science in the arts, music, manufacturing, transportation, or in consumer products for the home). Design and creation of technology is called *engineering*. There is overlap between science and technology, especially as that technology forms the instruments and tools of science and these tools depend upon, and are applications of, the laws of the natural sciences.

Observing. Examining or monitoring the change of a system closely

Glossary

and intently through direct sense perception and noticing and recording aspects not usually apparent on casual scrutiny.

Classifying. Systematic grouping of objects or systems into categories based on shared characteristics established by observation.

Measuring. Using instruments to determine quantitative aspects or properties of objects, systems, or phenomena under observation. This includes the monitoring of temporal changes of size, shape, position, and other properties or manifestations.

Interpreting Data. Translating or elucidating in intelligible and familiar language the significance or meaning of data and observations.

Inferring. Reasoning, deducing, or drawing conclusions from given facts or from evidence such as that provided by observation, classification, or measurement.

Communicating. Conveying information, insight, explanation, results of observation, or inference of measurement to others. This might include the use of verbal, pictorial, graphic, or symbolic modes of presentation, invoked separately or in combination as might prove most effective.

Controlling Variables. Holding all variables constant except one whose influence is being investigated in order to establish whether or not there exists an unambiguous cause and effect relationship.

Developing Models and Theories. Created from evidence drawn from observation, classification, or measurement, a model is a mental picture or representative physical system of a phenomenon (e.g., a current in an electric circuit) or real physical system (e.g., the solar system). The mental picture or representative system then is used to help rationalize the observed phenomenon or real system and to predict effects and changes other than those that entered into construction of the model. Creating a theory goes beyond the mental picture or representative model and attempts to include other generalizations like empirical laws. Theories often are expressed in mathematical terms and use models in their description (e.g., kinetic theory of an ideal gas, which could use a model of particles in a box).

Glossary

Hypothesizing. Attempts to state simultaneously all reasonable or logical explanations for a reliable set of observations, stated so that each explanation may be tested and, based upon the results of those tests, denied. Although math can prove by induction, science cannot. In science, one can only prove that something is not true. Accumulated evidence can be used to corroborate hypotheses, but science remains mainly tentative.

Predicting. Foretelling or forecasting outcomes to be expected when changes are imposed on (or are occurring in) a system. Such forecasts are made not as random guesses or vague prophecies, but involve, in scientific context, logical inferences and deductions based on (1) natural laws or principles or models or theories known to govern the behavior of the system under consideration, or (2) extensions of empirical data applicable to the system. (Such reasoning is usually described as "hypothetico-deductive.")

Index of Micro-Units by Subject

Physics

Motions and Forces

Translational Kinematics

Grade 9	Grade 10	Grade 11	Grade 12
914(a) p. 4	1010 p. 5	1117 p. 6	1210 p. 6
915 p. 4	1021(a) p. 5		
923 p. 5			

Gravitational Force: The Law of Universal Gravitation

Grade 9	Grade 10	Grade 11	Grade 12
914(b) p. 19	1014 p. 19	1122 p. 19	1236 p. 19

Dynamics: Newton's Laws of Motion

Grade 9	Grade 10	Grade 11	Grade 12
916 p. 11	1011 p. 11	1119 p. 12	1213 p. 12
918 p. 11			

Conservation of Momentum

Grade 9	Grade 10	Grade 11	Grade 12
917 p. 14	1012 p. 14	1121 p. 14	1234 p. 14

Rotational Kinematics

Grade 9	Grade 10	Grade 11	Grade 12
920 p. 8	1015(a) p. 8	1118 p. 8	1212 p. 8
	1016(b) p. 16		

Elastic and Frictional Forces: Electric Forces Between Atoms and Molecules

Grade 9	Grade 10	Grade 11	Grade 12
921 p. 24	1018(a) p. 24	1120 p. 24	1237 p. 24
922 p. 24	1021(b) p. 24		

Rotational Dynamics and Angular Momentum

Grade 9	Grade 10	Grade 11	Grade 12
935(b) p. 16	1016(a) p. 16	1126 p. 16	1235 p. 16

Electric Force: Coulomb's and Gauss's Laws

Grade 9	Grade 10	Grade 11	Grade 12
943(b) p. 21	1033 p. 21	1148 p. 22	1252 p. 22
	1039(a) p. 21		

Physics

Electromagnetism: Moving Charges, Magnetic Forces
and Changing Magnetic Fields

Grade 9	Grade 10	Grade 11	Grade 12
945 p. 26	1034(a) p. 26	1149 p. 26	1249 p. 26
946 p. 26	1035 p. 26		

Conservation of Energy and the Increase in Disorder

Heat, Internal Energy, and the Kinetic Theory

Grade 9	Grade 10	Grade 11	Grade 12
925 p. 34	—	1140 p. 34	1238 p. 34

Work, Kinetic Energy, Potential Energy, Field Energy, and the
Conservation of Energy

Grade 9	Grade 10	Grade 11	Grade 12
935(a) p. 28	1026(a) p. 29	1141 p. 29	1248 p. 29
936 p. 28			

Heat, the Transfer of Thermal Energy, and the Second
Law of Thermodynamics

Grade 9	Grade 10	Grade 11	Grade 12
937 p. 31	1026(b) p. 31	1138 p. 31	—
		1144 p. 32	

Interactions of Energy and Matter

The Wave Model: Water Waves, Seismic Waves, Sound and Light

Grade 9	Grade 10	Grade 11	Grade 12
919 p. 37	1015(b) p. 38	1127 p. 38	1229 p. 38
950 p. 37	1018(b) p. 38	1128 p. 38	
	1036(a) p. 38		

Electrical Insulators, Resistors, Conductors, Semiconductors, and
Superconductors

Grade 9	Grade 10	Grade 11	Grade 12
944 p. 46	1034(b) p. 46	1147 p. 47	1250 p. 47
			1257 p. 47

Quanta: The Discreteness of Atomic and Molecular Energy

Grade 9	Grade 10	Grade 11	Grade 12
949(c) p. 44	1039(b) p. 44	1129 p. 44	1253 p. 44
			1254 p. 45

Physics

Photons, Electromagnetic Waves, and the Electromagnetic Spectrum

Grade 9	Grade 10	Grade 11	Grade 12
949(b) p. 41	1036(b) p. 41	1151 p. 41	1251 p. 42

Chemistry

Structure and Properties of Matter

Solids, Liquids, and Gases: Empirical Laws and the Kinetic Theory

Grade 9	Grade 10	Grade 11	Grade 12
908 p. 60	1022 p. 60	1113 p. 60	1201 p. 60
909 p. 60			
929 p. 60			

Mixtures, Elements, and Compounds

Grade 9	Grade 10	Grade 11	Grade 12
910(a) p. 51	1024 p. 51	1110 p. 52	1203 p. 52
928 p. 51		1111(b) p. 52	
930 p. 51			

Molecules: Their Structure, Interactions, and Physical Characteristics

Grade 9	Grade 10	Grade 11	Grade 12
924 p. 58	1043(a) p. 58	1136 p. 58	1227 p. 58

Chemical Formulas and Chemical Bonds

Grade 9	Grade 10	Grade 11	Grade 12
963 p. 56	1042 p. 56	1109 p. 56	1219 p. 56
	1043(b) p.56		

Elements, Atoms, and the Periodic Table

Grade 9	Grade 10	Grade 11	Grade 12
961 p. 53	1040 p. 54	1133(b) p. 54	1255 p. 54
964(a) p. 54	1041 p. 54	1135 p. 54	

Hydrocarbons, Polymers, and Organic Macromolecules

Grade 9	Grade 10	Grade 11	Grade 12
957 p. 62	1047 p. 62	1146 p. 62	1205 p. 62
965 p. 62			

Chemical Reactions

Mass and Number Conservation in Chemical Reactions

Grade 9	Grade 10	Grade 11	Grade 12
931 p. 64	1028 p. 64	1111(a) p. 64	1202 p. 64
964(b) p. 64			

Chemistry

Energy Transformations in Chemical Reactions
Grade 9	Grade 10	Grade 11	Grade 12
942 p. 65	1029 p. 66	1112 p. 66	1220 p. 66

Oxidation/Reduction, Acid/Base, and Radical Reactions
Grade 9	Grade 10	Grade 11	Grade 12
958 p. 67	1044 p. 68	1155 p. 68	1226 p. 69
959 p. 68	1051 p. 68	1156 p. 68	
960 p. 68			

Chemical Reaction Rates
Grade 9	Grade 10	Grade 11	Grade 12
967 p. 70	1052 p. 70	1154 p. 70	1225 p. 71
968 p. 70			

Catalysts and Enzymes
Grade 9	Grade 10	Grade 11	Grade 12
969 p. 72	—	—	1221 p. 72
			1222 p. 72

Structure of Atoms

The Nuclear Atom and Its Components: Electrons, Protons, and Neutrons
Grade 9	Grade 10	Grade 11	Grade 12
943(a) p. 74	1038 p. 74	1133(a) p. 75	1256 p. 75
949(a) p. 74			
962 p. 74			

Nuclear Fission and Fusion
Grade 9	Grade 10	Grade 11	Grade 12
966(c) p. 79	1059 p. 79	1161 p. 79	1247 p. 80

Radioactivity and Its Applications
Grade 9	Grade 10	Grade 11	Grade 12
966(a) p. 81	1057 p. 81	1104 p. 81	—

Nucleons and Isotopes
Grade 9	Grade 10	Grade 11	Grade 12
—	1056 p. 77	1134 p. 77	1246 p. 77

Biology

Biological Evolution

Biological Classifications: Their Basis in Evolutionary Relationships

Grade 9	Grade 10	Grade 11	Grade 12
901 p. 111	1001 p. 111	1101 p. 112	1208 p. 112
	1055 p. 111		

The Processes of Evolution: Mutation, Recombination, and Natural Selection

Grade 9	Grade 10	Grade 11	Grade 12
903 p. 113	1002 p. 114	1103 p. 114	1216 p. 114
904 p. 113			

Natural Selection and Its Evolutionary Consequences

Grade 9	Grade 10	Grade 11	Grade 12
905 p. 108	1003 p. 108	1105 p. 108	1215 p. 109
907 p. 108			

The Molecular Basis of Heredity

Heredity, Traits, Genes, Chromosomes, and DNA

Grade 9	Grade 10	Grade 11	Grade 12
902 p. 103	1004 p. 104	1152 p. 104	1206 p. 105
	1005 p. 104		

The Behavior of Organisms

Organisms, Stimuli, Receptors, Nervous Systems, Responses, and Behavior

Grade 9	Grade 10	Grade 11	Grade 12
911 p. 124	—	1160 p. 125	1217 p. 125
912 p. 125			1218 p. 125

The Cell

Cell Structures That Underlie Cell Functions

Grade 9	Grade 10	Grade 11	Grade 12
932 p. 86	1025 p. 86	1159 p. 86	1228 p. 87
933 p. 86	1054 p. 86		

Cell Chemistry: Metabolism, Catalysts, and Photosynthesis

Grade 9	Grade 10	Grade 11	Grade 12
934(a) p. 89	1053 p. 89	1158 p. 89	1223 p. 889

Biology

DNA, RNA, and Genetic Engineering

Grade 9	Grade 10	Grade 11	Grade 12
—	1050 p. 92	1153 p. 92	1207 p. 92

Matter, Energy, and Organization in Living Systems

Energy Flow Within and Between Living Systems

Grade 9	Grade 10	Grade 11	Grade 12
952 p. 97	1048(b) p. 97	1145 p. 97	1224 p. 97
953(a) p. 97			

Cell Sources, ATP, and the Utilization of Energy

Grade 9	Grade 10	Grade 11	Grade 12
—	1049 p. 94	1157 p. 95	1242(a) p. 95

The Interdependence of Organisms

Cycles in the Biosphere and Energy Flow Through Ecosystems

Grade 9	Grade 10	Grade 11	Grade 12
953(b) p. 117	1030 p. 117	1142 p. 117	1243 p. 117
954 p. 117	1048(a) p. 117		
	1048(c) p. 117		

Organisms, Ecosystems, and Population Growth: Interrelationships and Interdependencies

Grade 9	Grade 10	Grade 11	Grade 12
955 p. 120	—	1143 p. 120	1242(b) p. 120
956 p. 120			1244 p. 121

Earth/Space

The Origin and Evolution of the Earth System

Interactions Among Ecosystems: Earthquakes, Volcanoes, Mountains, and Plate Movements

Grade 9	Grade 10	Grade 11	Grade 12
906 p. 151	1017 p. 151	1107 p. 152	1211 p. 152
913 p. 151	1019 p. 151	1137 p. 152	
	1045(b) p. 151		

Origin and Age of Earth: Rock Sequences, Fossils, and Radioactive Dating

Grade 9	Grade 10	Grade 11	Grade 12
966(d) p. 149	1013 p. 149	1106 p. 149	1233 p. 149
	1046(a) p. 149		

Evolution of Life, Bacteria, and Algae, and Oxygen in the Atmosphere

Grade 9	Grade 10	Grade 11	Grade 12
934(b) p. 153	1006 p. 153	1102 p. 154	1209 p. 154
	1007 p. 154		

Energy in the Earth System

Convection in Earth's Mantle, Atmosphere, and Oceans: Their Sources and Effects

Grade 9	Grade 10	Grade 11	Grade 12
910(b) p. 138	1020 p. 139	1115 p. 139	1204 p. 139
940 p. 138	1023 p. 139	1150 p. 139	1239 p. 139
948 p. 138	1031(b) p. 139		

Heat from Within Earth and Heat from the Sun

Grade 9	Grade 10	Grade 11	Grade 12
926 p. 131	1008 p. 131	1125 p. 132	1230 p. 132
938 p. 131	—	1139 p. 132	1231 p. 132
939(b) p. 131			
947 p. 131			
949(d) p. 131			

Global Climate: The Sun's Energy and the Influence of Dynamic and Static Factors

Grade 9	Grade 10	Grade 11	Grade 12
927 p. 141	1031(a) p. 141	1116 p. 141	1241 p. 142

Earth/Space

Earth's Internal Energy Sources: Radioactivity and Gravitational Potential Energy

Grade 9	Grade 10	Grade 11	Grade 12
939(a) p. 135	1058 p. 135	1108 p. 135	1245 p. 135
966(b) p. 135			

Geochemical Cycles

Movement of Elements and Compounds Among Earth's Reservoirs

Grade 9	Grade 10	Grade 11	Grade 12
941 p. 145	1027 p. 146	1114 p. 146	1240 p. 146
	1032 p. 146		
	1045(a) p. 146		

The Origin and Evolution of the Universe

Evidence and Theories to Explain the Evolution of the Universe

Grade 9	Grade 10	Grade 11	Grade 12
949(e) p. 156	1046(b) p. 156	1132 p. 156	1214 p. 137

Gravitation, Star Processes, and the Formation of Elements

Grade 9	Grade 10	Grade 11	Grade 12
951 p. 159	1009 p. 159	1123 p. 132	1232 p. 159
	1037 p. 159	1124 p. 152	
		1130 p. 159	
		1131 p. 159	

Index of Micro-Units by Number

B = Biology   C = Chemistry   E = Earth   P = Physics

Micro-Unit	Subject / Page	Micro-Unit	Subject / Page	Micro-Unit	Subject / Page
901	B 111	942	C 65	1009	E 159
902	B 103	943(a)	C 74	1010	P 5
903	B 113	943(b)	P 21	1011	P 11
904	B 113	944	P 46	1012	P 14
905	B 108	945	P 26	1013	E 149
906	E 151	946	P 26	1014	P 19
907	B 108	947	E 131	1015(a)	P 8
908	C 60	948	E 138	1015(b)	P 38
909	C 60	949(a)	C 74	1016(a)	P 16
910(a)	C 51	949(b)	P 41	1016(b)	P 8
910(b)	E 138	949(c)	P 44	1017	E 151
911	B 124	949(d)	E 131	1018(a)	P 24
912	B 125	949(e)	E 156	1018(b)	P 38
913	E 151	950	P 37	1019	E 151
914(a)	P 4	951	E 159	1020	E 139
914(b)	P 19	952	B 97	1021(a)	P 5
915	P 4	953(a)	B 97	1021(b)	P 24
916	P 11	953(b)	B 117	1022	C 60
917	P 14	954	B 117	1023	E 139
918	P 11	955	B 120	1024	C 51
919	P 37	956	B 120	1025	B 86
920	P 8	957	C 62	1026(a)	P 29
921	P 24	958	C 67	1026(b)	P 31
922	P 24	959	C 68	1027	E 146
923	P 5	960	C 68	1028	C 64
924	C 58	961	C 53	1029	C 66
925	P 34	962	C 74	1030	B 117
926	E 131	963	C 56	1031(a)	E 141
927	E 141	964(a)	C 54	1031(b)	E 139
928	C 51	964(b)	C 64	1032	E 146
929	C 60	965	C 62	1033	P 21
930	C 51	966(a)	C 81	1034(a)	P 26
931	C 64	966(b)	E 135	1034(b)	P 46
932	B 86	966(c)	C 79	1035	P 26
933	B 86	966(d)	E 149	1036(a)	P 38
934(a)	B 89	967	C 70	1036(b)	P 41
934(b)	E 153	968	C 70	1037	E 159
935(a)	P 28	969	C 72	1038	C 74
935(b)	P 16	1001	B 111	1039(a)	P 21
936	P 28	1002	B 114	1039(b)	P 44
937	P 31	1003	B 108	1040	C 54
938	E 131	1004	B 103	1041	C 54
939(a)	E 135	1005	B 104	1042	C 56
939(b)	E 131	1006	E 153	1043(a)	C 58
940	E 138	1007	E 154	1043(b)	C 56
941	E 145	1008	E 131	1044	C 68

Continued

Micro-Unit	Subject / Page	Micro-Unit	Subject / Page	Micro-Unit	Subject / Page
1045(a)	E 146	1128	P 38	1213	P 12
1045(b)	E 151	1129	P 44	1214	E 157
1046(a)	E 149	1130	E 159	1215	B 109
1046(b)	E 156	1131	E 159	1216	B 114
1047	C 62	1132	E 156	1217	B 125
1048(a)	B 117	1133(a)	C 75	1218	B 125
1048(b)	B 97	1133(b)	C 54	1219	C 56
1048(c)	B 117	1134	C 77	1220	C 66
1049	B 94	1135	C 54	1221	C 72
1050	B 92	1136	C 58	1222	C 72
1051	C 68	1137	E 152	1223	B 89
1052	C 70	1138	P 31	1224	B 97
1053	B 89	1139	E 132	1225	C 71
1054	B 86	1140	P 34	1226	C 69
1055	B 111	1141	P 29	1227	C 58
1056	C 77	1142	B 117	1228	B 87
1057	C 81	1143	B 120	1229	P 38
1058	E 135	1144	P 32	1230	E 132
1059	C 79	1145	B 97	1231	E 132
1101	B 112	1146	C 62	1232	E 159
1102	E 154	1147	P 47	1233	E 149
1103	B 114	1148	P 22	1234	P 14
1104	C 81	1149	P 26	1235	P 16
1105	B 108	1150	E 139	1236	P 19
1106	E 149	1151	P 41	1237	P 24
1107	E 152	1152	B 104	1238	P 34
1108	E 135	1153	B 92	1239	E 139
1109	C 56	1154	C 70	1240	E 146
1110	C 52	1155	C 68	1241	E 142
1111(a)	C 64	1156	C 68	1242(a)	B 95
1111(b)	C 52	1157	B 95	1242(b)	B 120
1112	C 66	1158	B 89	1243	B 117
1113	C 60	1159	B 86	1244	B 121
1114	E 146	1160	B 125	1245	E 135
1115	E 139	1161	C 79	1246	C 77
1116	E 141	1201	C 60	1247	C 80
1117	P 6	1202	C 64	1248	P 29
1118	P 8	1203	C 52	1249	P 26
1119	P 12	1204	E 139	1250	P 47
1120	P 24	1205	C 62	1251	P 42
1121	P 14	1206	B 105	1252	P 22
1122	P 19	1207	B 92	1253	P 44
1123	E 132	1208	B 112	1254	P 45
1124	E 152	1209	E 154	1255	C 54
1125	E 132	1210	P 6	1256	C 75
1126	P 16	1211	E 152	1257	P 47
1127	P 38	1212	P 8		